Tour of the City

Starting point: Upper Bridge / Old Town Hall
End: Schillerplatz

Route

Karolinenstraße
Geyerswörth Square
Geyerswörth footbridge / Geyerswörth Town Hall
round Geyerswörth Town Hall to the Old Canal
Bruckner footbridge
Old Canal
Am Kranen / Beginning of Kapuzinerstraße
Hasengasse
Austraße / An der Universität
Fleischstraße
Maxplatz
Hauptwachstraße / Grüner Markt
Neptune Fountain / Keßlerstraße / Wallenstein passageway to Lange Straße
Obstmarkt
Lower Bridge
Dominikanerstraße
Kasernstraße to towpath and back to Dominikanerstraße
Ringleinsgasse
Karolinenstraße
Roppeltsgasse
Vorderer Bach / Steps up to cathedral hill
Cathedral hill / square / New Residence / Old Court
Domstraße / top end of Obere Karolinenstraße
Michelsberg
Aufseßstraße
through Michelsberger monastery garden / steps to terrace
St. Michael's Monastery
St.-Getreu-Straße to Villa Remeis
Wildensorger Straße / Jakobsberg
Jakobsplatz
Maternstraße
Square by Carmelite Church
Kaulberg / Upper Parish Church
Eisgrube / Stephansberg square
St. Stephen's Hill down to Pfahlplätzchen
from Pfahlplätzchen back to Concordiastraße and Upper Mills
Upper Mill Bridge
Mühlwörth
Nonnenbrücke
Schillerplatz

A Day for *Bamberg*

Willy Heckel & Emil Bauer

A Day for Bamberg

A Tour of a World Heritage City

Translated by Rosemary Neberle

Verlag Fränkischer Tag

Front and back covers inside: 2 maps taken from
Bamberg map No. 317 published by Bollmann-Bild-
karten-Verlag, Rilientalplatz 1, 38108 Braunschweig

Pictures:
p. 8: last photo of Emil Bauer and Willy Heckel
together on the occasion of the presentation of the
book "Sandkerwa" (Photo: Ronald Rinklef).
p. 9: photo by Waltraud Heckel.
All other photos by Emil Bauer.

© 2003 Verlag Fränkischer Tag, Bamberg
All rights retained
5. updated print (new edition)
Production: Maren Ullrich
Edited by: Monika Beer, Anna Elisabeth Stein
Translated by: Rosemary Neberle
Layout: Erich Weiß
Reproduction and printing:
creo Druck & Medienservice, Bamberg
Printed in Germany
ISBN 3-928648-98-5

ntroductory Reflections

"What – yet another Bamberg book?" That was exactly how the author reacted, when he was asked if it was not high time for him to reach for his pen again. Without thinking it over, his spontaneous answer was: No, no further Bamberg book by him. His stock of praises for the town had already been exhausted in three books on the same theme, as co-author of several other works and in a whole host of essays etc. If he ignored that, he would be bound to run the risk of just repeating and reformulating thoughts he had long since put to paper. He neither wants to nor is he able to devote one more eulogy to Bamberg, especially after the success of his book "Bamberg – Dream City of the Germans". In any case, such a short time after publication of that book, he feels incapable of finding any new angles on the town. Absolutely nothing has happened that can have changed the role of the town or its self-image. If he should ever write another book about Bamberg, then it would have to be completely different to the last one. The reader has a right to expect that.

That was the key: a different Bamberg book! But what sort of book? What is lacking? Chance came to his rescue. In the course of his work, he was given to understand, with an expression of gratitude, that the brochure he had written and published for the municipal tourist office decades ago had helped over half a million visitors to Bamberg. It was a tour of the town with the title: "Through a thousand years in a few hours" and proved to be a highly welcome source of information for visitors trying to get to know Bamberg. So the author said to himself, why not write a long guided tour, especially as it gives you yourself sheer joy to guide both friends and strangers through Bamberg.

The idea gripped him more and more. It intensified into the idea that it should be a very special guided tour, not just a stringing together of stops on a sight-seeing tour, not just a mere collection of dates, facts and comments. If he does it at all, then the tour should also be a really good look at, an assessment of, the town he is presenting and also a dialogue with those who want to get to know it. But will there be enough people who want to read it?

The answer: one should try it, particularly as it is absolutely conceivable, the Bamberger himself could gain something from such a book, too. It would give him practical help to guide other people himself, something every local person is called upon to do at some time or other. And as far as potential readers who already know Bamberg are concerned and who for that very reason would like to have a continual reminder of Bamberg – yes, of course, how could one better serve them than to wander through the town with them in their imagination?

The author became more and more sure of himself. If he could succeed in giving the "Guided Tour of the City" (or whatever else the book might be called) a sort of story as underlay, then it would make it more readable than guidebooks and similar works generally are. And if the text was accompanied by pictures in unison as often as possible, then it would be ridiculous if such a book did not make its way to the reader. Particularly, as, apparently, the demand for Bamberg books has not been covered by far.

The author then spent a long time, really long, reflecting on how, as a town guide, one could best disclose one's ideas of a town like Bamberg to the reader. Should one approach the subject from the outside and then, with a steady intensification, reach the essential part, the climax, the heart only at the very end? Or would it be better, like the Bamberg Rider as it were, to jump into the saddle at once and to look around from his point of view? The author turned down those ideas. Innate boredom would have been the result of both suggestions – in the first half of the book for the first, in the second half for the second. The only remaining possibility was to follow the principle the well-known Echternach "spring procession" teaches one: for every three steps forward, you spring back two, three steps forward, two back... That would give him the chance to

Town Knight in Geyersworth Castle

Mitoraj sculpture on the Lower Bridge

repeat things often, to recapitulate, to consolidate details already related. Idea rejected! Such a tour would mean an underestimation of the person being guided, thinking him stupid.

Finally the author came to the conclusion that one had to look for a special way of approaching the subject, a way specially tailored for Bamberg. That meant beginning the tour at a place that would be suited, like the overture of an opera, to allow the basic melody and leitmotif to be discernible from the start. In addition the place ought to whet the appetite for what was to follow, in just the same way that the starter of a menu with many courses arouses one's curiosity as regards what is to follow (and as to the capacity and creativity of the cuisine). Where in Bamberg is there such a spot, a – to quote an Italian example – Piazzale Michelangelo like in Florence? Starting from there, you foresee the wonder of the city to come, without it divulging all its secrets in advance.

There is such a place: the Old Town Hall in the middle of the river. That is where we should meet for our tour, on a sunny October morning, when the light flows in honeylike yellow through the town, or in early summer after a shower of warm rain, when the town looks freshly washed and combed and the paving shines as if it had been polished. The time is not so important, the main thing is we have our starting point first of all.

But have we got our guide, too? No, not yet, so we shall have to look for him, or wish for him so hard that he will begin to take shape quickly. The author suggests it should be a layman, not a professional, please! Preferably rather like in Victor Zobel's delightful book, "Selige Bierreise", about a merry beer tour, in which a button maker from the Rhineland leads the way to the Bamberg beers and not, as one would expect, a master brewer. Professional guides – as everyone knows – too easily fall into the habit of reeling off facts, into a routine of

Detail of the Crucifixion group on the Upper Bridge

Sculpture in E.T.A. Hoffmann Square

texts learnt by heart and into a maze of dates that the tourist cannot get through.

Our city guide should therefore be a man (or a woman) from another profession. This would be more realistic for Bamberg anyway, for most of, if not all, the town's guides have in fact been properly trained, but they are not full-time. They just have a sheer passion for guiding. Let us simply say, our guide is to be a journalist. That has less to do with autobiographical links to the author but rather is to show the author's intention of including reflections and developments concerning the present in our tour of Bamberg. And which profession would be better suited to express an opinion about that than that of the journalist?

It only remains to find a name for our man. Do not let us make it too difficult, let us simply say, his name is Jakob Kern. That is a good name, one that does not sound strange to Bamberg ears. If there should be someone of the same name and who could be confused with our guide moreover,

then we can deal with it like in films: any similarity with living persons is unintentional.

And his audience, the group to be guided? With one exception for purely literary reasons, we do not want to sketch any particular characters nor have to justify any specific identities. Everyone who reads the book should be able to imagine that he is walking with Kern himself, that he can ask him questions, have this and that explained, he can contradict, be sceptical or even smile at the occasional exuberant exaggeration.

So that is the end of a preface we felt was necessary to introduce the book. We – that is the signatory, the author of the manuscript, and Emil Bauer, who has once again illustrated the text with photos – would like to extend you a warm invitation to join a guided tour of Bamberg which will certainly be somewhat out of the ordinary. Follow us inconspicuously, so to speak, through the "dream city".

Willy Heckel
(Preface to the first edition)

ith Journalistic Ease

When Willy Heckel makes the fictitious guide, Jakob Kern, say in the book, that he is not really the right person to convey the beauties of the town to the tourists, because he is a journalist, then of course that is an autobiographical allusion. Willy Heckel was a journalist and that with body and soul. With the wording, he is an editor who knows the town fairly well, Kern testifies of course to a touching modesty – if one equates him with the real Heckel. To wit, hardly anyone knew the town as well as Willy Heckel.

Willy Heckel is no more. He died on 13th July 2001. The memory of an exceptional journalist remains with us. As head of the Bamberg local editorial office, he decisively shaped the *Fränkischer Tag*. There remain, too, his books, like this one, about Bamberg. Willy Heckel was proud of the

fact, that this declaration of love devoted to his home town was such a success. Published in 1989, "A Day for Bamberg" went into the second edition only three years later, the third with minor updating appeared in 1994 and the fourth edition in 1997. Now the fifth edition, again with a careful updating of text and pictures, takes the changes in the cityscape, that occurred around the turn of the millennium, into account. And this new edition emphasizes the importance that fell upon Bamberg when UNESCO included the Old Town of Bamberg in its World Heritage list.

As head of the Bamberg local editorial office, Willy Heckel was an important personality in the town and known beyond its boundaries. He combined two good journalistic qualities: he had a critical mind and possessed the talent of being able to formulate his ideas with journalistic ease. And he had a partner of kindred spirit, both in his job as newspaper reporter and as the author of books: the photographer Emil Bauer. He is always a meticulous observer of all that happens in the town. On the basis of his long years as photographer, he can make use of a host of comparisons.

Willy Heckel and Emil Bauer have one thing in common: their calling was journalism involving events of the day. But they always identified themselves with their town and its people, even more: their love of Bamberg was and is clearly recognizable in their work. Shortly before his death, Heckel had begun to write a Bamberg book that was to be, so to speak, the quintessence of his two illustrated books, "Bamberg – Dream City of the Germans" and "A Day for Bamberg". His knowledge of the history of the city, bundled up in the book, "Bamberg in the 20th Century", was to be incorporated into the new book, too. Sadly that was not to be.

Willy Heckel makes his fictitious city guide, Jakob Kern, explain the Bambergers' motives for their love of the town as follows: the town simply pleases them, it is their "dream city". One cannot express it more beautifully than that!

Siegfried Hännl

W. Heckel, E. Bauer and the mayor, Herbert Lauer

*E*mil Bauer was born in Bamberg in 1928. He studied chemistry for some semesters, then turned his hobby, a passion for photography, into his profession and became a press photographer, first with the *Bamberger Volksblatt* and *St. Heinrichsblatt* and from 1954 with the *Fränkischer Tag*. No other photographer has portrayed Bamberg and its citizens so often: Emil Bauer is *the* portraitist of Bamberg in the second half of the 20th century.

In the over fifty years, in which he has been working with his camera, he has never been content with just a mere recording of current happenings. Many of his pictures are photographed still lifes, stories in black and white and colour: humorous, enigmatically ironic, marginalia of both the everyday and great events. His skill as a craftsman and creative power as an artist reach their culmination in his pictures of town and landscape. His numerous books are among the best of their genre. Bauer photos have appeared in over 150 books. The *Fränkischer Tag* publishing house brought out many titles – mainly together with Willy Heckel, whom he has known since he was a boy and with whom he has worked for almost 40 years. In 2001 he was awarded the city medal.

*W*illy Heckel was born in Bamberg in 1926. He served four months in the war, followed by four years as a prisoner of war in Yugoslavia. A report he did for the wall newssheet of a Belgrade camp met with such good response that it encouraged him in his decision to become a journalist. After his return in 1949, he studied journalism and history in Erlangen and Bamberg. From 1952–54 he had a post as trainee with the *Fränkischer Tag*, in 1954 he became a member of the Bamberg local editorial office, headed it from 1959 and lastly was chief editor as well. He retired in 1989.

Willy Heckel wrote about life in Bamberg in all its facets all the 37 years of his working life and since. His initials WH were to be found under numerous reports and commentaries, of publications outside Bamberg as well. As author and co-author he wrote several Bamberg books and brochures with a large circulation. His Polyglott Guide and, together with Emil Bauer, several other titles enjoyed particular success. He was also a lecturer at the Bamberg Otto Friedrich University and at the municipal adult education centre, as well as a member of its governing board. In 1992 he received the city medal.

The Old Town Hall in the middle of the Regnitz

Old Town Hall – A Good Place for an Overall View

Jakob Kern, whose group had been told to meet on the Upper Bridge at 10 o'clock, waited until the clock had struck ten. Then he emerged from the archway and saw the eleven participants gathered by the parapet of the bridge between town hall and Crucifixion group. He gave a courteous bow and tried to hide the stage fright he always had when he had to introduce himself to a new group behind a smile. This did not quite work and he said: "Ladies and gentlemen, I'm your Bamberg guide."

Kern told them his name and that he was not really the right person for them, with the emphasis on "really". He was a journalist, editor to be more exact, but somebody who knew the town relatively well. For this reason he was confident he could make the town, where he had worked for many years, known to others. Now he did manage a smile with the remark that he did not want to make the mistake of "real" town guides – that of bombarding his group with dates and names, which nobody could remember anyway. Dates and names were important, but they alone did not impart the essence of history. If he did mention them, then only if absolutely necessary to put them in the picture in the well over one thousand years of Bamberg's history. Kern sensed the agreement he found in his group, especially from a lady in the middle. One could see from the expression on her face, more than on the others', that she was looking forward to the guided tour about to begin.

Kern stuck to his principles: "I also want to give up the use of superlatives," he said. "But if I should do so, then please tell me. I don't want to and I'm not going to talk you into believing that Bamberg is the most beautiful city, that nowhere can you live so well as here, that here you will find art expressed at a level of perfection to be found nowhere else: the town as the most magnificent of backdrops, the most wonderful sculpture, the largest old town ensemble in Germany, if you count the number of listed buildings – just a moment, I really could say that, because it can be verified, namely about 2,300 protected objects. Let's forget everything else I mentioned. Everyone may and must decide for himself, what is the loveliest, the most sublime and most precious."

So how does he want to present Bamberg then? Well, to be sure, as a very old and beautiful town and, perhaps a surprise, as a very important city; a city whose citizens have tried hard to preserve their heritage, to look upon it as the "gift of a millennium". He wants to make clear that the past is not felt as a burden here, something to cast off in favour of the more modern, the more practical, the easier to look after. No, the Bamberger is happy to live in an old town, in a town where the present is simultaneously the past, where both mingled into a feeling for life, that makes you calmly confident – something many towns cannot succeed in, on the contrary they make you ill.

That must be the explanation why the Bambergers did not part with the old around them, rather left it just as they had received it. They were thinking of their town less as an example of a thousand-year-old urbanity, to be preserved quasi as testimony, just as in geology outcrops remain as testimony, to what has disappeared. Their motives are much simpler: they just like the town, it is *their* "dream city".

Kern was clearly making an effort to use the subjunctive form in his now finished prologue. That was to make it clear that he was not speaking out of exuberance or local patriotism, but with the detached judgment of one convinced by experience. Besides the cunning old devil knew that it was, at least at the beginning of a tour, better to understate than to lay it on too thick. The lady, whose expression showed she was looking forward to Bamberg, had already nodded several times in agreement with Kern's fundamental remarks. Kern assumed she had come straight from Munich. Her smart but casual costume in traditional look looked suspiciously like one from "Lodenfrey", the specialists in loden fashion. Very chic.

But now, Kern thought, it was high time to begin the tour. He added that from now on he did not want to use the term *guided tour* any more but rather call it a *walk through the town*, a sort of day's journey through the "dream city". His role was just to call attention to what there was to see, to find out and to admire. "You'll like it, this *day for Bamberg*," he said with great certainty. (To give the reader the feeling that he is taking part in this walk, we are going to use the present tense from now on instead of the past.)

Kern explains why he is beginning the walk on the Upper Bridge. "Seen from here, much of Bamberg's basic pattern is clear," he says. First the river is part of this basic pattern: the Regnitz and its two arms, which the Bambergers call the right and the left one respectively. The bridge we are standing on leads over the left one. The river splits the town into parts but does not divide it – an important difference. It arranges the town in parts and gives it the chance to take on the brightness of the flowing water and extend it to the land. "Take a look at the former fishermen's settlement of Little Venice down there and you'll know what I mean."

Here by the Old Town Hall, the "Bridge Town Hall", you can clearly see that Bamberg is marked by two topographically completely different situations. To the west, the part of the town on the hills spreads itself over the relatively steep foothills of the Steigerwald Forest, which fall to the Regnitz. This is called the *ecclesiastical town*, because this was where the ecclesiastical dominants with the cathedral in the middle lay. On the other side of the Regnitz the *bourgeois town*, with the marketplace as its centre, grew in the meadows of the valley.

If he was a "proper" town guide, Kern says with a smile, he would now tell the following story: "Ladies and gentlemen, you can see that the Old Town Hall, that we're standing in front of, is neither in the hilly part of the town nor in the bourgeois town. No, it stands on a man-made island in the river. Why? Well, because bishop and townspeople quarrelled about where it should stand. And because they couldn't agree, at least they agreed on a compromise – and placed the town hall in the river. And it still stands there today."

Kern tells his group, he cannot avoid unmasking this lovely story as just a legend. It sells itself so well to visitors but is not verified. It is probable that the Old Town Hall was built *on* the Upper Bridge, because, as first crossing over the left arm of the Regnitz, it had always been a place where the citizens met. Here they traded, bought and sold. It is documented that fixed stalls were there as early as the 13th century. The decision to integrate the town hall into the bridge was therefore both understandable and wise, for the Bambergers could not have placed their town hall closer to the people (in contrast to many a municipality today, which locates its administrative centre in the open countryside and then trusts its citizens will somehow find it).

By the way, Kern adds, the Bamberg bishop did not have to quarrel with the mayor about the right site for the town hall. As ruler, it lay in his power to decide such a matter alone.

One final point, while we are standing here on the Upper Bridge in front of the Old Town Hall, a third fundamental factor can be ascertained: that Bamberg is a Gothic town clad in a Baroque wrap, says Kern and immediately realizes that this has not been understood. "Ladies and gentlemen," he explains, "when we have a chance later to look down on the town from above, then you'll easily recognize that the town's ground plan is Gothic: that means not keeping to right angles, sharp-cornered forks and junctions, streets and alleys that meander like streams, houses built close together with high, steep roofs. But this, in its outline and shape, Gothic town bought itself a completely new wardrobe in the 17th and above all in the 18th century, namely a Baroque one and Baroque of the finest. I can show it to you on the Old Town Hall, the best example."

The town hall, says Kern, is Gothic in core: a narrow, structural timber frame, a high, steep saddle roof, two rows of dormers, one above the other. Between 1744 and 1756, the master builder, Michael Küchel, converts it into Baroque, wraps it in a new mantle, that completely changes the earlier more modest character of the 15th-century building, gives it a new personality, the elegant, bright and playful that now suits it so well.

The late-Gothic half-timbering is plastered over and Johann Anwander paints frescoes onto

Rococo to perfection: Town Knight and balcony on the tower of the Old Town Hall

the plaster in 1755 – what do we mean by paints: he showers the walls with them. The tower above the old archway gets a new wardrobe, too, is given Rococo appliqué, delicately wrought balconies, that seem to grow out of the stone. Above them are the coats of arms of the city (on the hill side) and of Bishop Franz Konrad von Stadion (town side) in playful cartouches – masterpieces by Bonaventura Mutschele, a name Kern mentions for the very reason that it sounds so melodious: Bonaventura Mutschele. And then the Baroque remodellers set a shiny black slate roof with curved hips and a dashing little belfry on top of the tower. "You see," says Kern, as if he is telling a secret, "this is what happened all over the town, that is now Baroque in appearance – unless we climb up on its roof or scratch at the façades."

Kern calls this brilliantly successful conversion, which was promoted with the help of tax incentives, the first example of redevelopment in Bamberg. He says so, even though it largely amounted to nothing more than the decorative and did not actually make anything better or cure anything, improvements which are gener-

Upper Bridge: Crucifixion group with Evangelists

Upper Bridge: St. Nepomuk and Upper Parish Church

ally implied by redevelopment. The second phase is still going on, as can be seen in exemplary fashion with the town hall on the bridge, namely in Anwander's frescoes. They are still in such a good state of preservation, only because the town council commissioned the Bamberg painter, Anton Greiner, to recreate them between 1960 and 1963.

Then Kern leads his group past the Crucifixion group made by Leonhard Gollwitzer in 1715. Its pious pathos is in stark contrast to the humble stoop of the saint so often portrayed on bridges, St. Nepomuk, by the opposite parapet. When they look at the Nepomuk statue, Kern asks them to include the soaring chancel of the Upper Parish Church on the first hill above the river in the background. Not just because both together make such a picturesque composition, but rather to shed light on the Janus face of Man in the Gothic Age: here in the foreground the stooped, maltreated man of bondage, over there, in the boldness of the chancel, an indication of the other spirit of Gothic times, the longing for nearness to God. It finds its most perfect expression in the cathedral built, to the limits of the technical possibilities of the age,

Upper Bridge: St. Nepomuk and Old Town Hall

Frescoes on the Old Town Hall (above);
the painted putto with a "real" leg (below)

to reach up to heaven (and waiting for later generations to finish building it).

Kern points out, he says as a contrast programme, the trompe l'œil architecture in the Anwander frescoes on the long walls of the town hall, the pillars and pedestals, which the beholder is supposed to think are really there and not just painted – Baroque tricks as to be found on many 18th-century buildings. That one of the putti on the wall of frescoes facing the town has really grown a leg, a limb you could grasp hold of, Kern calls a "feigned deception".

Kern tells his group that the council chamber on the first floor is used only for official functions now. Among other uses, the Old Town Hall used to be home to the municipal adult education centre, the Volkshochschule, until it could move into the converted electricity power station by the right arm of the Regnitz. The town auditing office then took its place in the town hall, not perhaps particularly fitting in such a bright and important building, but it was a good idea in that it did not cause a stream of visitors and no emission at all! The ideal use, that does not hurt the building's fragile structure but suits its genius loci, was not found until 1995: the museums of the City of Bamberg have since then shown the Ludwig Collection under the title: "The Splendour of Baroque". It is a collection of faïences and porcelain here on permanent loan. The museum offices are housed alongside the precious products from Strasbourg and Meißen.

Kern knows, as he had found out before the tour, that a reception had been held in the Rococo Chamber, the town's "parlour" and former council chamber, the evening before. He speculates that the room might have been aired and tidied for the museum visitors. Yes, indeed – the room is open. The group is delighted by the brightness of the room: windows on three sides with fresh, billowing net curtains fluttering in the wind, fantastically lovely views through them, over the river and its banks and up to the cathedral, over the ridges of the steep Gothic roofs, crooked with age. Right under the windows on the west side is Dominikanerstraße, as narrow as a gorge, and to the north, almost on a level, the smiling face of St. Kunigunde on the Lower Bridge.

The beauty of the town wafts through the room, so much so that the group almost overlooks the sumptuous Rococo furnishings, the stucco with its shell ornamentation, the sopraporta, the oil paintings by Anwander depicting the four cardinal virtues, the blue-grey faïence stove, the coats of arms of the mayors. Kern tells his people: "If you come on an official visit with an association or delegation, the town will be pleased to receive you here. As a rule, they like to splash out." And he adds that they occasionally serve the wine called "Ewig Leben", which means "eternal life", to their visitors. That is not a pious wish, but the location of a vineyard in Randersacker near Würzburg. "That's nice," says the lady in the smart loden costume and gives the impression that she would not mind if someone served her a

"The Splendour of Baroque": lady with Moor

Rococo Chamber in the Old Town Hall

glass of "Ewig Leben" right now, even though it is still morning. A pretty woman, thinks Kern (and guesses her to be about forty).

The group leaves the town hall and goes out to the west end of the bridge, from where a lovely view of the Lower and Upper Mills upstream opens up. The first antiquarian bookshops and antique shops. The whole of Karolinenstraße right to the foot of cathedral hill is full of them: furniture, prints, clocks, pewter, faïences, pottery, earthenware, antique jewellery, paintings, books, a lot of art, hardly any junk. No wonder, says Kern, that, since 1996, there have been Bamberg Antique Weeks held at the same time as the Wagner Festival in Bayreuth.

Just before the bridge ends in the flat beginning of Karolinenstraße stands the Meranier Fountain, surmounted by a mighty eagle with wings spread, on the right – a memento of a house that died out long ago. They once had great power in the Upper Main region. They also provided one of the most important Bamberg bishops:

View from the Upper to the Lower Bridge

Ekbert von Andechs-Meranien, the builder of the third cathedral, the one we have today, in 1237, a prince of the Church who was the brother-in-law of two kings and who – unjustly though – was accused of being an accessory to the murder of a third. He had a sister and a niece who were both to be canonized later. These were St. Hedwig and St. Elizabeth.

Were the Upper Main Andechs-Meranier related to the house of the same name, who had their seat on the Holy Mount of Old Bavaria, in Andechs Monastery above the Ammersee lake, asks the lady in the smart Munich look. Kern: "The same family." Well, I never, he thinks to himself, good thinking.

Kern leads his group on left to the Geyers-wörth square. But first he shows them No. 6 Karolinenstraße, a lovely house with a statue of St. James the Younger on the façade. Kern "has" them stop at the splendidly restored "Brudermüh-le", once the mill of the monastery brothers. From this spot the participants of the walk have an unhindered view of a large building complex that Kern describes as the former Franciscan Monastery, that was secularised long ago. The Bavarians took it from the Church and eventually restored it at great expense. Kern goes on to say, with a bitter note in his voice, that the church of the Francis-can Monastery had been made short work of and simply demolished after secularization. It was only much later, during roadworks, that its foundations saw the light of day for a short time again (and the skeletons of those who had been buried there).

Kern now turns his group's attention to the Brothers' Mill. He arouses greater interest by adding that a miracle happened to the building. The group is curious. "The monastery mill," says Kern, "became the first town waterworks once its function as a mill had come to an end. That was more than a hundred years ago. Now the one-time waterworks have changed miraculously and are a ..." – Kern makes a dramatic pause to let his listeners solve the riddle for themselves – "Now it's a wine tavern," resounds in chorus, for you can see its new function from the hotel and restaurant sign. A Franconian Cana.

The sculpture of the Assumption of Mary on the mill's corner facing Schranne square is with certainty Baroque and Baroque of the best, prob-

Meranier Fountain by the Old Town Hall

Statue of St. James, No. 6 Karolinenstraße

Baroque Assumption of the Virgin Mary on the corner of the Brothers' Mill

ably the work of Gollwitzer, who also created the Crucifixion group on the Upper Bridge. Kern thinks, if you keep quiet, you can hear the wings of the angels carrying Mary up to heaven flapping. But the driver of a car who cannot find a place to park gives vent to his annoyance by hooting his horn.

Kern asks his group to go on to the Geyersworth footbridge, a bridge of wooden planks but surely more beautiful than the iron construction which preceded it. But still not beautiful enough for the Bambergers, because the bridge is their proscenium box, from where you can view one of the most impressive architectural scenes in Bamberg: the Old Town Hall floating like a ship at anchor in the foaming waters of the Regnitz.

Kern does not even need to describe the sight. It conveys itself: the Regnitz, the speed of its flow increased by the weirs of the Lower Mills, roars under the bridge full of high spirits towards the bow of the town hall plinth, on the tip of which the so-called Rottmeisterhäuschen, the bailiff's house, seems to balance most precariously. You can see the Gothic origins of the town hall in its half-timbering, which was uncovered quite a few decades ago and its framework repainted. The curators of historical monuments are not so happy about that. They consider making the half-timbering visible has torn a hole in the Baroque mantle and would prefer it to be patched, or in this case plastered over. Kern comes to the end of this chapter by remarking that there is plenty of scope for a good discussion about half-timbering in Bamberg and where it should be shown or where preferably covered up. He also remarks, with a note of query, whether it is mere chance that the youth welfare office is now housed in the old bailiff's house.

The group still cannot tear itself away from the beautiful view. Fascinated, they watch how the town hall, standing in the river, tames the "white water" of the Regnitz, quietens it down and makes it more gentle. It follows the principle of divide et impera and splits the river into two almost equally strong watercourses which can only come together again once they have passed the town hall. The river then goes on its way, purposefully and with only one more weir further down by the old spinning-mill in Gaustadt to hinder it, and flows into the Main. If he, Kern, has spoken of white water,

Lower Mills: temporary addition and grill

White water canoeist by Geyersworth Bridge

21

View of Geyerswörth Castle, now municipal offices

Tower of Geyerswörth Castle

Renaissance Chamber in Geyerswörth Castle

then rightly so, for here, between the Lower Mills and Old Town Hall, annual canoe slaloms take place; you see the wires, from which the poles for the gates are hung, stretching across the water.

"We must go on, ladies and gentlemen!" Kern urges his people and invites them into the Geyersworth town hall at the east end of the footbridge. He takes this opportunity to remark that Bamberg's town halls are not really town halls at all. The town hall on the bridge, as already explained, was built over a trading place and bridge tower, the New Town Hall on Maxplatz square was built as a priests' seminary by Balthasar Neumann, the so-called Technical Town Hall with various offices of the municipal planning and building departments is located in buildings of the old hospital in Sandstraße and Geyersworth Town Hall, that he wants to look at next with them, was a prince bishop's castle with a, at that time, famous garden of which the spacious rosebeds next to it are a reminder – above an underground car park by the way.

On top of the Geyersworth underground car park

Geyersworth Castle, it is presumed, was built by Erasmus Braun from Nuremberg around 1585, so is a Renaissance work. He was also the master builder responsible for the council chamber in the Old Court up on the cathedral hill. Prince Bishop Ernst von Mengersdorf ordered the building of the castle; his splendid coat of arms adorns the large gateway. The group is only listening with one ear. They are once again enraptured, this time by the atmosphere of the inner courtyard of the former castle. Kern tells them that a three-day wine festival takes place in the courtyard annually at the end of June or beginning of July. In the meantime it has become a tip among Franconia's wine festivals from Klingenberg to Zeil. "The Franconian Wine-growing Association serves its wines over there," says Kern pointing to the arcades in the northeast corner of the courtyard. The original coat of arms from the side of the Old Town Hall facing the hills has been installed there to protect it from the effects of the weather. The group looks at the Town Knight depicted in the cartouche of the coat of arms. He is bent at the hip like a z and they conjecture he is still a bit tipsy from the smell of wine at the last Geyersworth festival, because he poses so gracefully beside his shield in spite of his heavy suit of armour.

Fountain in the courtyard of Geyersworth Castle

View of the Mill District from the tower of Geyerswörth Castle

Opposite, an old-looking fountain splashes as softly as a whisper, Virginia creeper grows rampant over the courtyard walls. Of course, says Kern, plays and concerts can also be performed here. The group can well imagine what a wonderful venue it is, as there is almost complete quiet. Not even the noise of the Regnitz penetrates the thick walls.

Kern asks if the eleven ladies and gentlemen in his group would like to climb the Geyerswörth Tower with him. "We'll have a fabulous view up there in the lantern that crowns the roof," he says pointing it out. "Shall we?" Of course they want to. The key is fetched in no time; it is deposited at the Tourist Information right next door during working hours.

The tower's flight of stairs is narrow: a spiral staircase in the stone tower, at the top, under the roof, a wooden staircase suspended from the wooden frame of rafters. The last bit is as steep as a slanting ladder. As there are seldom people coming in the opposite direction, there are hardly any jams or crushes. No comparison with Old Peter in Munich or the Strasbourg Minster, where the streams of visitors going up and down often "seize up", which causes claustrophobia even in those of robust nature. Besides there are only 132 steps up to the lantern.

Talking animatedly, the group begins the climb. Soon it becomes noticeably quiet. The only communication is with their own breathing. It gets lighter the last few metres. There is the lantern already. Just ten, twelve people have room in it. Kern opens the bolted windows, lets the sunny morning in and says: "Now take a look out! Isn't it wonderful?"

The group is delighted. Over there the ecclesiastical city spreads itself over the seven hills, a townscape that is as lovely as it is dramatic with the cathedral in the middle, flanked by the mighty mass of buildings of the New Residence, the former monastery of St. Michael's, the Upper Parish Church, St. Stephen's and other towers. Nothing needs to be said to make the beauty of this picture understandable.

Kern is silent, too. He keeps quiet on principle between the stops on his tours. Continuous talking, in his opinion, prevents the visitors from perceiving what lies by the wayside. Up here in the lantern of the Geyerswörth tower, he just says: "You should remember that over a thousand years have worked on this picture, shaped it, added this, removed that and yet one fits the other, nowhere is there a sharp-edged break, rather it is *one* work of art as a whole. Now you can understand it more easily than if I had said it to you down below, that Bamberg is one single work of art. It was

with good reason that it was put on the UNESCO World Heritage list in 1993."

And Kern adds: "If only we could succeed in building so harmoniously in our modern towns and their various districts, in positioning the dominating features with a sure hand and in adding one to the other, without the large and the mighty stifling the small and unprepossessing – just as successfully as it has happened here!" Kern carefully shuts the windows of the lantern, makes sure that the bolts sit tight and climbs down again with his group. The eleven people behind him feel as if they have been given a present.

Before the group leaves the inner courtyard of Geyerswörth Castle, Kern tells them that the Renaissance chamber in the south wing is, after the Rococo chamber in the Old Town Hall, the town's second reception room. A further remark deals with the strange name "Geyerswörth". 'Wörth' stands for an island, 'Geyer' for a family, who once had property here: the island of the Geyers.

View of the "city on the hills" from Geyerswörth Castle tower

Bruckner Bridge across the old King Ludwig Canal

Around the Market – Sketches from the Town of the Burghers

Back in the street once more, the end of Geyerswörthstraße, the group turns right. Kern leads them round Geyerwörth Town Hall. After a few metres it becomes more than clear that 'Wörth' really is an island, formed by the left arm of the Regnitz and the old Ludwig Canal. As a forerunner of the Main-Danube Canal, which was finished in 1992, the old canal made navigation between Danube and Main possible for about a hundred years from the middle of the 19th century onwards. It was an old dream to link the river systems of the great European rivers, Rhine and Danube, with each other. Charlemagne dreamt of it, his Fossa Carolina remained a fragment. The Bavarian king, Ludwig I, however, managed to have the canal dug from Kelheim on the Danube to the Main near Bamberg, 172 kilometres long with exactly 100 locks. The hundredth lies just down there by the fulling-mill, though not visible from here. Kern tells the group they will see

it later, if they keep going that long. Here, at the rear of Geyerswörth Castle, they are standing by the last (most northern) stretch of the canal, by its confluence with the Regnitz, that it has "made use of" for quite a stretch above Bamberg.

Whether the canal makes sense, is asked. Kern thinks dreams have something about them of being unreal. Definitely the "royal canal" achieved hardly any importance in transport politics. It came too late. When, in 1846, it reached its full length and barge navigation was possible for the first time, it had already been overtaken, so to speak, by the railway. As far as the new canal is concerned, Kern asked them not to overlook the signals for Europe that it without doubt set. And particularly the city of Bamberg profited from the building of the canal. The extension of the right arm of the Regnitz into a major waterway was reason for laying out green promenades along the banks, right through the whole town from north

Chapel in No. 10 Upper Bridge

Gothic houses beside the King Ludwig Canal

to south, something nobody would like to do without today. Besides it was possible to make the Old Town safe from flooding. He will be talking about that later.

The group agrees: the Old Canal has remained an idyllic spot. On the opposite bank stands a lovely town house with lancet windows on the first floor, an indication that the house once possessed a Gothic private chapel. This splendid building for example, No. 10 Upper Bridge, has undergone a complete and lavish restoration at great expense, some of it public funding, says Kern drawing special attention to it. This comment serves him as an excuse to point out the so-called Bamberg-Model – a municipal financing scheme. It was intended as an incentive to carry out redevelopment measures in the Old Town, doing justice, as far as possible, to the conditions for the preservation of historical monuments. The Bamberg Model has completely fulfilled the task intended for it, and indeed that in a double sense:

not only did it cover the additional costs of the restoration of individual objects in accordance with the requirements of preservation, but it also became contagious. Nearly every successful case of restoration was cause for the neighbour on the right or on the left or even opposite to tag along, too. So Old Town redevelopment with the effect of a bush fire? "Exactly," says Kern.

One reaches the other side of the canal by crossing the footbridge named Bruckner after the carpenter who built it. It is a sort of wooden Rialto Bridge. The group turns left and walks along the canal, under the Upper and Lower Bridges, until it joins the Regnitz. Through the east arch of the Upper Bridge, the Lower Bridge is revealed as flat as a board. "How could the town council approve that bridge?" grouses one of the group. "You don't like it, do you?"

Kern becomes a little unsure, says: "No, I don't like it, but I've got used to it." And then he tells them just how this type of bridge came about

"Bridge Town Hall": the horn of plenty, a detail in the frescoes by Johann Anwander

Lower Bridge: Igor Mitoraj's large sculpture of a centurion

and not any other. Its forerunner was not particularly beautiful either, even though it did have basket arches. It was blown up by the Germans at the end of the war in 1945, like all the around twenty Bamberg bridges and footbridges. This was to stop the American troops entering, without any success of course. To succeed it, a plain, straightforward bridge, quasi the prototype of the bridge, was suggested to the town council two decades later: just a board, but a concrete board, because that was the building material of the day for bridges.

Kern goes on to say, that this was a clear argumentation for the town council, they liked the concrete board. Now it lies there, but it turned out rather thick, contrary to their expectations. It does not vibrate (from the aesthetic point of view), looks more like a massive railway sleeper and is a beam in the eye for many Bambergers. Kern: "Since then I've got into the habit of no longer

being satisfied with just hearing rhetorical grounds for municipal building intentions. With words you can present almost anything plausibly. It is better if you ask for a model and then take a long look at it and from all sides." It is clear that Kern is trying to make a correct judgment. To follow this up, he adds the comment that the new Lower Bridge has proved itself functionally. Its heavy, broad parapets, for example, are an open invitation for the high-spirited to do a balancing act on them. On Saturdays, when the young people of Bamberg hold a flea market on the Lower Bridge, they can spread out their bits and pieces on them. Secondly, since 2001, there has been a relative improvement in the aesthetic question, since the impressive Mitoraj sculpture has found its place here, with substantial support from donations by the townspeople. In the meantime the group has reached the east bank of the Regnitz. This spot is called

Lower Bridge with horse and wagon and Little Venice behind

The pleasure boat, "Stadt Bamberg", alongside the quay, "Am Kranen", and Old Town Hall

The "Stadt Bamberg" with the Sand District and St. Michael's Church in the background

Am Kranen, "By the crane", though correctly it should be "By the cranes", for there are two, both with a mushroom-like roof.

Kern thinks his group will want to know why there are cranes here, where only passengers boats tie up. Do they heave the passengers on board with the hook of a crane? "A clear case," says Kern, "Bamberg's old harbour was here in the Middle Ages and right up to the first years of the 20th century." Photos exist that show the river full of boats, moored so close together that it almost seems to be a bridge of boats. From this spot, Albrecht Dürer embarked on his journey to the Netherlands. Here the river boatmen and wine merchants called Messerschmitt unloaded their tuns of wine. From here emigrants set out on the long journey to America in the 19th century. Today only the two passenger boats, "Stadt Bamberg"

and "Christl", take their guests on board from the old harbour. Occasionally an iron lighter anchors over there by the small island that divides the Regnitz and canal just before they rejoin.

Nevertheless, Kern emphasizes, Bamberg has kept its position as a port. A new harbour was built farther north, near where the Regnitz flows into the Main, in 1912. There was large-scale extension into a state harbour in 1962. In better times it has had a turnover of about one million tons of freight transported by water. It is the turntable of Upper Franconian traffic and so part of Bamberg's future.

The group enjoys the lovely view across to "Leinritt", a street name that recalls its one-time function as towpath on the left bank of the Regnitz: horses on the towpath pulled the river barges with long ropes uphill. Downwards they moved

on their own. Over there stands the former Dominican Monastery – Kern announces they will
be visiting it later – higher up St. Michael's Monastery sends its greeting into the valley, a large,
spreading complex of buildings, that reminds one
a little of the Prague Hradschin. Indeed there are
quite a few similarities to Prague. But Bamberg, as
Kern stresses, is not called the Franconian Prague
but the *Franconian Rome*, above all because of the
seven hills it is built on – like Rome. Also because
Bamberg, though not an eternal city, is a holy one.
Or should be.

Kern draws his group a little closer round
him, as the traffic is rather loud at this spot. He
clearly wants to make sure that the following
comment is really understood by all of them:
"Bamberg," he says, "has not just remained a port,
it has also become a university town again with
a good 8,000 students at the moment. If I say
'become again', then that means that Bamberg did
have its own university from the middle of the 17th
century. After secularization in 1803, the Bavarians took it away in favour of Würzburg. Now it
has returned after a long road to satisfaction for
the wrong done. Even though there is a new campus in Feldkirchenstraße, it has returned to the
Old Town, where it once had its place and where
it has been given and is still getting plenty of room
to spread and develop. Bamberg gives it everything
that it cannot otherwise use itself!"

Kern lists them: the city's former "Wedding
House", a municipal building for citizens' celebra-
tions, on the opposite side of the street. Then
there are the buildings of the old Academy and
Jesuit College, several town houses in Austraße,
Fischgasse and Kapuzinerstraße, a former gram-
mar school, the old fire engine garage, the last
remaining tower of the town's fortification, a
complete maternity hospital, the former Dominican church and lastly the old slaughterhouse here
by the river. "Ladies and gentlemen, nothing is
too good for our university!" That does not even
sound ironic.

Of course all the buildings he listed had to be
converted and restored before they could be put
to their new use, measures welcomed by the city
of Bamberg. To verify this remark, Kern takes the
historical slaughterhouse right next to the group
as an example. A mighty stone ox, an unmistak-

A Baroque jewel in the Schulgasse alleyway

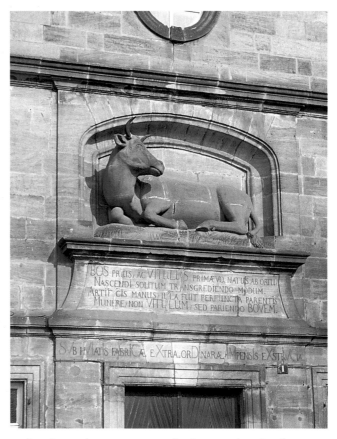

Ox above the entrance to the former slaughterhouse

Winter night; looking from "Am Kranen" towards St. Michael's

Inner courtyard of No. 1 Kapuzinerstraße

able sign that it really was a slaughterhouse in former times, lies in a niche in the façade of the Baroque building. He seems completely unmoved by the fact that, in the meantime, it has become the faculty library for history and geography studies. "Which library other than this can allow itself an ox as house sign?" asks Kern and takes delight in this "superlative".

He adds that the location of the slaughterhouse by the river was certainly not just a matter of chance. They surely must have thrown the scraps from slaughtering straight into the river. The fish must have grown fat on them and the fishermen no poorer. Imagine such an "ecological balance" in the present day, says Kern. Similar things happened at the Old Hospital farther down the river. It has been converted into a posh 4-star hotel. It was built in 1789, the year of the French Revolution. When a surgical clinic was added in 1900, where today, by the way, the municipal archives are housed, its ideal location right by the river was praised in the inauguration document. This allowed them to let the sewage flow direct into the Regnitz. "Don't worry, this kind of waste disposal doesn't happen any more," Kern feels obliged to add.

The group goes on into Kapuzinerstraße, named after a former Capuchin monastery, that also fell victim to secularization and disappeared without trace. Kern stops at house No. 5 Kapuzinerstraße and suggests they now take a look at an old house from the inside. Then they can see and experience that Little Venice is no sham façade just for the tourists, but still lived in today. He has got permission therefore to visit the house of the fishermen's guild.

The building actually consists of three houses with a little courtyard between, where fishing and shipping equipment is displayed on the walls, under that the rudder of a Main barge. The office of the "Bamberg Fleet" is in the house at the front. By "fleet" we mean the two passenger boats, the "Stadt Bamberg" and "Christl". The name of the owner is Fritz Kropf; in the rear building lives a relative with the same surname, Baptist Kropf. The rear house is also the front house for it stands right on the river and its façade, characterized by wooden galleries, looks onto the water. A world in reverse? "No, a beautiful world," says Kern and

invites his group to walk through the open passageway of the rear house and right down to the Regnitz. Then they will realize that it is also a front house and furthermore how wonderful it is to live here by the river. "By the way, now we're right in the middle of Little Venice." The group is enchanted.

Little Venice is a former fishermen's settlement. Like the merchants of Venice with their palaces, so the Bamberg fishermen built their houses right by the water in what is now called Little Venice, not on the such-and-such canal but by the river, on "their" roadway. Tiny little gardens with a brilliant display of flowers line the almost 300-metre-long row of houses; black, flat-bottomed boats bob up and down on the slightly ruffled waters of the Regnitz, washing and a few metres of fishing net hang on the line to dry, a group of cyclists in light-coloured clothes wave across from the old towpath. An idyllic scene.

"Doesn't the constant risk of flooding make you pay dearly for this idyllic spot?" one of the

High-water mark from the year 1784 in Königstraße

38

group asks. Kern can put their minds at rest: in no way. Flooding does not occur any more in Little Venice or anywhere else in the parts of the Old Town that the left arm of the Regnitz flows through. A high-water barrage in Bug, right at the south end of the town, takes care of that. If the Regnitz is carrying too much water, it is raised and thus forces the river to send its "overload" into the right arm of the Regnitz. It is deep enough and its embankments so high that the whole town remains dry. But this has only been the case since the 1960s, when the Regnitz was built into a major waterway through the town itself. Before that flooding made life extremely difficult – even today the numerous high-water marks in the town give you an idea of that. In the worst floods that occurred in past centuries, the whole of Bamberg, except the hills, was submerged.

The guild chamber of the Bamberg fishermen's and bargees' guild is on one of the upper floors of the "rear-front" house. The guild itself has remained an imposing organization with age-old statutes and even older traditions, even though it is an indisputable fact that its members now "keep their heads above water" with gravel and sand dredging rather than fishing and barge navigation. In the anteroom to the chamber, Frau Kropf shows them the treasures belonging to the Bamberg fishermen: Baroque procession staffs, a no less Baroque St. Peter, the garlands that each member has to wear on his head, when he is allowed to carry his guild's treasures in the great processions of the year, the Corpus Christi one above all, through the town, a great honour each time. The sweat of the wearers has faded the garlands. Finally there is a very high quality portrayal of fishing on the Sea of Galilee. From the guild chamber there is a fantastic view of the cathedral, that seems almost near enough to touch. Below lies the river shining in the sun.

Kern urges his people on their way. The group thanks the Kropfs, a large Bamberg family clan, warmly. They go up Hasengasse, an alleyway so narrow that, if someone is coming the other

"Rich catch" in the house of the fishermen's guild

The university in the inner city with the last remaining city tower

way, two people cannot walk side by side. They soon reach Austraße, a lovely street with fine houses. It has undergone a slow regeneration and has been, so to speak, newly discovered, ever since it was made into a pedestrian precinct and so no longer suffers from the strain of motor traffic. It reminds one of the Quartier Latin with its street cafés.

The university has lodged itself in this inner city area, has spread itself so widely that one can definitely speak of a university quarter. Part of the former Jesuitenstraße has therefore been renamed An der Universität, meaning "By the university". That is all right by the Bambergers. They both accept and promote the intention, with the rebirth of the university, of deliberately offering a university right in the town, the antitype of the university campus in the open countryside. If the university makes use of buildings in the Old Town, then a sensible redevelopment of the Old Town can be pushed ahead at the same time. This consideration plays a great role. Kern assures his group that the Bamberg university concept is appreciated by the students, too. You can see that from the fact that far more young people study in Bamberg than was ever planned for. In Bamberg, one can mainly take subjects in the humanities and economics, namely Catholic theology, education, philosophy, psychology, language and literature studies, history and geography studies, as well as social sciences, economics and informatics.

Kern strolls on through the university quarter with his group. First they visit the inner courtyard of the former theological college. It was built by Johann Leonhard Dientzenhofer at the turn of the 17th to 18th century. From the Jesuit monogram IHS in the suggestion of a sopraporta above the entrance, you can see that the beginnings of the old Bamberg university lay in the education of priests. The Council of Trient had imposed that as a condition. The inner courtyard, open to the sky above, is a place of quiet in comparison with busy Austraße. The top of a mighty tree spreads like an umbrella over the benches. A nice place to just sit and meditate between lectures. The Faculty of Catholic Theology is located in the former college building. Kern tells them one can visit the old natural history specimens gallery in the north wing. It is now part of the Natural History Museum that

Former Jesuit College

Renaissance portal, No. 7 An der Universität

Great Chamber in the Natural History Museum

is well worth a visit and not just because of its extensive and interesting collections. The museum is an exhibit in itself.

The university continues on the other side of the street. Language and literature studies have their home in the U 5 building (derived from the street and number: An der Universität 5). Kern shows them the magnificent Renaissance portal of what is now the faculty library and points out the house where the city physician used to reside, now a busy university building. He goes on into the so-called Burgershof, the seat of the public works office. The municipal civil engineering and building offices were housed there not so long ago, together with the fire brigade. Now the sciences "reign" here. The most striking part of the complex is a tower, in which the university chairs of language studies were set up. The tower, says Kern, is the last remaining one of the former fortification of the city. At this point he would like to tell them something about its defence.

Kern waits until the group has regathered closely round him. He remarks that, in spite of the tower they are standing by, Bamberg was never really a completely fortified city. It did actually have a city wall with towers and gates – you can see that very clearly in mediaeval pictures of the city – but the ring was either never completely closed or it did not meet the latest prevailing developments in technology. This was quite a different matter in the case of the so-called "north fortress" of the Bamberg ecclesiastical principality, Rosenberg Castle in Kronach, and the "south fortress", Forchheim. Thus Bamberg was always more picturesque rather than well-fortified. Consequently a war was never really waged over Bamberg. Nobody besieged or, more correctly, had to lay siege to the town. No barrage of artillery fire was set going from outside the walls and from inside nobody poured pitch through the machicolations or boiling water from the battlements over the enemy's heads.

The longest war over Bamberg was an internal disagreement, the so-called "Immunities War". What is understood by this term is the quarrel lasting for years between the burghers and those Bambergers who enjoyed the prerogative and privilege of living in an "immunity". These were districts exempt from taxation, responsible only

The castle bear "Poldi" in the Natural History Museum

to the bishop, but not to the city. This is why they could refuse, with success, to help with the costs of the fortification of Bamberg. The result: Bamberg remained a town almost incapable of its own defence. A town which foreign rulers could seize without great difficulty. Kern pauses and then goes on to say that, just because they could not defend themselves and never had to suffer besiegement, their inclination for war was never goaded into pure fury. That unholy rage usually encourages conquerors to react by smashing everything to pieces in the captured town.

It is true that the Bambergers were bled, Kern continues, their silver confiscated and their treasures stolen, war contributions demanded from them, hostages taken and now and then the town sacked, albeit with restraint, but the town did not suffer destruction – neither by the Hussites, who could be induced, by large payments, to turn back in the run-up battle, nor by the peasants who had forced their way into the town, nor by the imperial troops, neither by the Swedes, the French nor the Prussians. Two exceptions prove the rule, Kern

Prince bishop's coat of arms on the Maxplatz town hall

"Eye of God" on house No. 7 Hauptwachstraße

Baroque vase on the Maxplatz town hall

thinks. One was Margrave Albrecht Alcibiades von Kulmbach, who burnt down Altenburg Castle, and the second those Bambergers and the "defenders" who, in April 1945, thought one should blow up all the bridges in front of the advancing Americans.

Kern formulates the quintessence of his theory: "I don't want to make any contribution to the disarmament debate nor to put the case for pacifism, but doesn't it actually seem as if the Bambergers of past centuries through their defencelessness (and that contrary to their wish?), at the same time laid the preconditions for their town being able to survive just as it was?" Kern is pleased to see that the members of his group are thinking about this hypothesis of the interaction between the inability to defend oneself and the ability, just because of that, to stay alive. They go on discussing it while walking, via the Heumarkt square, the old hay market, and Fleischstraße, to Maxplatz. In passing, they ponder over the sensuous aura of Fernando Botero's "Reclining Woman with Fruit".

View of the square, Maxplatz, from the "House of the Parakeet" (Honer's department store)

Maxplatz is the largest square in the town centre and here stands the present-day town hall. It was built as a priests' seminary by the great master builder, Balthasar Neumann, from 1732 to 1737 and was used as such right up until 1927. The town took it over as town hall once the seminarists had moved into their new seminary building on the Heinrichsdamm embankment in 1928. Where once the dean, who was at the same time suffragan bishop, as was custom, had the say, the mayor now rules. The town council meets in the old refectory. Kern brings his discourse on the mutation of a seminary into a town hall to an end with the following sentence: "Whether the Holy Spirit is particularly close to the town council, because of the former godly use of its town hall, is a matter of dispute. Some say the town councillors are imbued with the Holy Spirit constantly, others think they lack Him." At this point the lady from Munich makes herself heard. "More respect, Herr

Kern!" she says, but, at the same time, makes it clear that she herself has more respect for he who is lacking in respect.

Maxplatz in its present form did not use to exist. It was inserted into the townscape through the demolition of the town's first parish church, the Old St. Martin's Church. It stood here for over 500 years. In 1804, during secularization, it fell victim to the pickaxe, which was on the rampage at that time. It sent a last greeting at the end of the 1960s, when the square was dug up, right down deep into the ground water, to make an underground car park. The foundations of Old St. Martin's came to light again, as well as the mortal remains of the Bambergers who had been buried in the church's graveyard throughout the centuries.

The town had the remains of its former fellow citizens collected and buried a second time in the new cemetery. "History is ever present in

Fresh from the market gardens in Bamberg and the surrounding countryside: Maxplatz vegetable stall

Grüner Markt: front of Raulino House

St. Martin's Church and Karstadt department store seen from the tower of Geyerswörth Castle

Bamberg, all the more so under the ground, where its traces survive longer anyway," says Kern and adds that, in his opinion, the practical syllabus for the Chair of Mediaeval and Modern Archaeology at Bamberg University will not run out of subjects.

"By the way, the whole lay-out of the square is a subject for public discussion again," Kern remarks and shows his group a bronze relief of the ground plan of the old, Gothic St. Martin's Church on the edge of the fountain in front of the entrance to the town hall. On the other side of the square is the monument to King Maximilian I of Bavaria who gave his name to the square. It used to be in the middle, but moved to the edge quite a long time ago. Max stands at the top, coated with green patina it is true, but in royal pose. It almost seems as if he is blessing the change in circumstances from his high pedestal – from the occupa-

tion of the prince bishopric and ecclesiastical principality of Bamberg in November 1802, then the dissolution of the ecclesiastical small state, right up to its incorporation into the later kingdom of Bavaria. It almost seems as if he is calling upon the figures below him for their silent testimony. At the feet of Maximilian stands no less a person than the founder, so to speak, of the "independent" Bamberg, Emperor Henry; Kunigunde, the Hohenstaufen king, Konrad III, who is buried in the cathedral, as well as Bishop Otto the Holy, are there too. Kern introduces all of them.

The daily market adds colour to Maxplatz. The market spreads across the square, a lovely and splendidly stocked market. The stalls overflow with the crops which market-gardeners in Bamberg and the surroundings grow. The gardeners, says Kern, used to be one of the most important trades in Bamberg with trading links right down

Statue of "Humsera" in Grüner Markt; this was the nickname of a well-known market woman

Jesuit saints in St. Martin's

Depiction of the legend of St. Martin in the church

to Munich and up into Thuringia. They were particularly famed for two agricultural products: liquorice, that Kern describes as an early form of chewing gum, and onions, from which the Bambergers get their nickname, "the onion treaders".

Hauptwachstraße runs along the south end of Maxplatz. Together with Grüner Markt and Obstmarkt, the old fruit market, it forms the most important street in the town centre. Today it is a precinct free of traffic and reserved for pedestrians only. In Baroque times it was Bamberg's main boulevard, beginning from Sees Bridge with its over-rich ornamentation with statues (its present-day replacement is Kettenbrücke) and continuing right up to the Old Town Hall and cathedral – a via triumphalis.

The elegant façades of the houses, for instance No. 7 Hauptwachstraße or the Raulino House opposite St. Martin's Church in Grüner Markt, are a reminder of the one-time splendour of the boulevard. And of course the façade of the church itself, consisting of two triumphal arches, one on top of the other. Kern specifically draws attention to it. St. Martin's Church was built as a Jesuit church from 1686 to 1693 by Georg und Leonhard Dientzenhofer. It later became the university church and, after Old St. Martin's was demolished, finally replaced that as parish church. With all the will in the world, one "cannot skip" St. Martin's, says Kern and invites his group inside.

A spacious, high interior in white and gold opens out, only at the far end, in the chancel, is there a gleam of pink light, like the sunrise on the horizon. Ex oriente lux? That cannot be true, for the choir is at the west end. So "sunset" at best. Larger-than-life figures in fluttering white robes with gold piping line the nave: Jesuit saints. Their Baroque appearance, imbued with life, should not disguise the fact that those members of the Society of Jesus, who were elevated to saints, died the wretched death of a martyr, most of them in the Far East, which they wanted to convert.

As a contrast to the Baroque sculptures, Kern shows them a late-Gothic pietà on the right side altar. She seems almost abstract in her moving simplicity. Christ, descended from the Cross, lies as stiff as a board on His Mother's lap. The work came from Old St. Martin's. Kern explains and

Neptune in his winter furs; the "Fork Man" covered in snow

tells them about the annual meeting of the town's two large statues of the Virgin Mary here in St. Martin's, on the occasion of the great procession in honour of Mary. The second figure is the one of Our Gracious Lady from the Upper Parish Church. The silent dialogue of the two statues is one of the inalienable fixtures of the Bamberg church year.

Before Kern leads his group outside to Grüner Markt again, he advises them to look up into the high dome. They notice at once, what Kern is getting at: the dome is only a painted illusion. The Baroque pattern is right in St. Martin's, too, for a Baroque church has to have a dome. On the other hand, there is the new altar for the officiation of Mass, a work by Paul Schinner from Nabburg. The folds of St. Martin's cloak flutter over the stone altar table. You can really touch and feel them: they are "there".

Back in Grüner Markt, the group turns right to "Gabelmann", the "Fork Man", a Baroque Neptune fountain, standing where Keßlerstraße turns off Grüner Markt. The imposing sea god used to

Waterspout on the Neptune Fountain

Portal ornamentation on the Wallenstein House

DAS HAVS STET IN GOT
TES HANT ZVM CAMEL IN
DER KESLERS GASSEN IST
ES GENAND · M·D·LXXXIX·

House sign on the "House of the Camel"

look across to the Old Customs House, a finely proportioned Renaissance building, which was badly damaged in the last days of the war, though its outer walls remained standing. In comparison with the years of need, 1945/46, people have changed their understanding of their architectural past. Today nobody would think of demolishing the ruins. But at that time it happened. At this point, Kern adds the remark that, of course, there were people in Bamberg, too, who were of the opinion that a few more bombs on the right spot would have done no harm. Then it would have been easier to adapt the town to the motor car. Kern: "Meanwhile even the very last citizen knows you can make all sorts of things out of Bamberg, but never a town suitable for cars – unless you demolish everything." The group murmurs approval.

Kern now has his "criticizing phase". He says, the discussion about the "furnishing" of the pedestrian precinct was conducted with great controversy, too. The citizens gave no peace until the so-called "Pipe Fountain", a modern fountain consisting of more than ninety curved steel pipes, was removed from its place in front of St. Martin's. Meanwhile not even the critics dispute the fact that the pedestrian precinct fits in. Only in the evening is it terribly empty and quiet, except for a few people still sitting by the Neptune Fountain. But that is a complaint that you hear from other towns, too.

Kern suggests a little detour into Keßlerstraße, where he shows them the very finely carved stone sign on No. 9, the "House of the Camel". Its pendant is the "House of the Elephant" over in Generalsgasse. Both house signs date from the second half of the 16th century. The Fork Man, with only his naked back in view from Keßlerstraße, is one hundred years younger.

The group uses the passageway through Wallenstein House to reach the Lange Straße, which is outside the pedestrian precinct. A pizza baker has his stand halfway along the passage. And how you can smell it. It is worth taking a look at the beautiful portal of Wallenstein House, comments Kern. The magnificent Baroque building – also called "House of the Chamber" – is Gothic in core. The high stepped gable towers up like an exclamation mark above the roofs of Lange Straße.

Bamberg's patron saint: statue of Kunigunde on the Lower Bridge

Kern urges them to hurry. It is midday already and he has reserved a large table for his group at the foot of Katzenberg in the "Sand District" on the other side of the river. Via Obstmarkt, with its view up the town side of the bridge to the Old Town Hall and part of the Baroque boulevard mentioned several times, they quickly reach the Lower Bridge. Kern stops once more by the statue of the saint and empress, Kunigunde, a work by Peter Benkert, made 1744/45. The group catches up with him. "What you see here," says Kern, "is only a copy." The original has long since been taken to St. James's Church for safety. It had been damaged several times. This included breaking her nose off, which made the statue's gentle, warm smile suffer terribly. The Bambergers have now accepted the copy, especially as the new Kunigunde has a smile just as beatific as the old one.

Kern makes a historical detour and recalls that the statue of the patron saint of the bishopric was once only one part of the sculptural ornamentation of the Lower Bridge. In 1784, in one of the worst floods in the history of the town along with the breaking up of the ice, the bridge, together with almost all the other Bamberg bridges, including the particularly richly ornamented Sees Bridge, collapsed. The statue of Kunigunde was saved. The figures of the emperor, St. Henry, and two other saints fell into the torrential river and disappeared without trace forever.

In contrast, Kern points out, when the right arm of the Regnitz was enlarged into a major waterway in the 1960s, parts of the sculptured figures of the Sees Bridge, which had collapsed on the same day, were dredged up from the sand of the riverbed after almost 200 years. These included part of the horse, on which the dragon slayer, George, had sat and even the goldplated tongue of the dragon that George, in never-ending action, had been stabbing to death on the bridge. The fragments recovered can be seen in the History Museum.

When Kern walks on towards Dominikanerstraße, it seems as if he is really bidding farewell to Kunigunde on the Lower Bridge. Asked if that is really so, he answers: "Please, believe me, when I say the Bambergers have an unbroken and heartfelt relationship with the lady up there. Kunigunde is the patron saint of the city." Which is the reason

a lot of Bambergers think it is thanks to the saint, that Bamberg came through the Second World War with relatively light damage; Kunigunde held her protective shield over the town.

"And that's really believed?" the lady from Munich asks. "Believed all right," says Kern and walks on.

It is of no matter in which inn Kern has booked a table for lunch for his group. May the remark suffice, that it was a restaurant in the Sand District and there are plenty of places to eat in Sand, like the grains of sand in the sea. That reminds me: this is the chance to make a mention of *the* celebration in the town, the Sand Church Fair. That must be made. Kern uses the time between the ordering and the serving of lunch for a digression into Bamberg cooking, whereby he stresses that there is not a "real Bamberg cuisine". Cooking in the town is Franconian with some local embellishments. Franconian highlights to delight the palate are to be found in the traditional meal known as a "Brotzeit", generally eaten at the brewery inns or outdoors. A typical "Brotzeit" is a large meat loaf with a delicious crust that is baked by the butchers. It has a misleading name, "Leberkäs", meaning liver cheese. To eat with it, the bakers have rolls, called "Weckla" in local dialect, on offer in never ending quantities.

Kern expressly draws their attention to the fact that people have the right to take their own "Brotzeit" with them into the brewery inns in the town. It is an unwritten law that, at the hours when it is usual to have a "Brotzeit", in the morning or afternoon between 4 and 6 p.m., you are allowed to buy your food at the butcher's and baker's. Then you can sit yourself in the inns to consume it, as if you had all the time in the world. You do not need to feel embarrassed about it, there is not even a cover charge. On the contrary, the landlord will bring you a plate and cutlery free.

A lunch speciality is beef with horse radish and cranberries. Apart from that, roast pork, in every variation, dominates the menu, with mugwort and a lot of caraway and crisp crackling – or as "Schäufela", a piece of pork from the shoulder. To go with the meat, potato dumplings, also called raw dumplings, are predominant as ever. In Bamberg the German word for dumpling is

6

"Schlenkerla" Inn

At the end of August every year: Sand Church Fair

Sand Church Fair with an Italian touch: two gondolas opposite Little Venice

Madonna on house No. 2 Sandstraße

"Kloß". You should not use the name "Knödel". That would be Bavarian. The most frequently used vegetables are savoy, in German "Wirsing" but pronounced "Wirsching" in dialect, red cabbage, spinach and beans, in May and June, of course, asparagus, which grows in sufficient quantities, particularly in the neighbouring places south of Bamberg. Something very special are the carp. They are eaten only in the months with an 'r' in the name, which is why you cannot find them on the menu now, in the summer months.

Kern cannot get round to adding something else to his appetizing remarks. This would have been a lecture on the Franconian frying sausage and its variations in the area between Coburg and Kronach in the north and Nuremberg in the south. He would have loved to have gone into the special case of the Bamberg onion sausage. But lunch is already being served. He says: "Mahlzeit", the south German version of "Enjoy your meal", and says cheers to his group with a glass of dark beer. He thinks they are the best group he has ever

had. To tell the truth, we must add that Kern has sat himself next to the good-looking lady from Munich. She is drinking a glass of Franconian wine, a dry Silvaner called "Escherndorfer Lump". That does not sound very ladylike, for "Lump" is a rogue, a rogue from the Eschendorf vineyards. With it she is eating so-called "blue tips", frying sausages simmered in a wine and vinegar stock. Between two bites, she asks Kern what he has actually got against Bavarians. His remark that one was not allowed to say "Knödel" for the dumplings, because that would be Bavarian, and even more the tone, in which he had said it, made one conclude that his relationship was troubled.

Kern replies that he has nothing whatsoever against Bavarians and Bavarian ladies. Otherwise how would he have sat himself next to one. If he keeps describing the Bambergers as Franconians, then this results from a Franconian instinct for self-preservation, in order not to be sacrificed to everything Bavarian. "Poor Herr Kern," says the lady and polishes off her "blue tips".

They all enjoyed their lunch, but now they are all a bit lethargic and tired. Kern knows from experience that, after lunch, he will have to sum up all his eloquence. So he heads for a spot that he thinks will wake his people up again. From Sandstraße he turns into Kasernstraße and goes to the end, right down to the west bank of the Regnitz, to "Leinritt", the old towpath.

Little Venice, that the group visited in the morning, lies opposite. Only when you see it as a whole, do you realize how picturesque the row of houses is, like a line of pointed, Gothic writing, almost no Baroque round curves among them except for one tiny house with a mansard roof exactly opposite. River and town make up one, a perfect picture. It is as if the group's tiredness has vanished.

Kern turns round and goes up Kasernstraße again. Before they reach Sandstraße, he turns left into the inner courtyard of the former Dominican Monastery. The secularised Dominican Church, a late-Gothic hall church, was the domicile and concert hall of the Bamberg Symphony Orchestra for a good forty years until the middle of the 1990s. A highly unusual concert hall, but not one that allowed the world-famous orchestra unmarred playing or the audience optimal listening. The

Cloisters of the former Dominican Monastery

acoustics played pranks on both. Kern remembers the glass roof suspended over the podium. It was supposed to stop the pianissimi "getting lost" in the vault of the Gothic chancel. In contrast, the acoustic conditions are the very best in the "Symphony by the Regnitz", as the new concert and congress hall just under a kilometre downstream is called, enthuses Kern. It was not until after the move there in September 1993, that the Bambergers could really hear their "Bambergers" properly. And they went wild with enthusiasm.

That reminds me, says Kern, in the meantime, the university has annexed the Dominican Church with similar enthusiasm. The monastery buildings behind were restored a long time ago, too. Their Baroque character shines in its original splendour once more – to the advantage of the townscape and the public employees who work there in the state structural engineering and waterways offices. How far would you have to look to find lovelier office rooms? The old monastery library on the second floor has been made into a lecture room, which can also be used by the public. The owner, the Free State of Bavaria, is very generous in this respect. That is a good thing, says Kern, because it was precisely the Dominican Monastery that was made to suffer so much in former times. The church was used as a granary and a military store, the monastery buildings as barracks for a Bavarian battalion, hence the unfitting name of the street, Kasernstraße, the "barracks street". The only building improvement during this terrible period of misuse of former monastery property was the erection of a latrine for the battalion.

Before the pretty lady from Munich can lodge a protest, Kern announces that he now wants to

"Symphony by the Regnitz", the concert and congress hall

Little Venice

say a few sentences about the relationship between the Bambergers and the Bavarians. Definite is the fact that the Bambergers were not asked if they wanted to become Bavarians, just as little as the Nurembergers and Würzburgers, the Bayreuthers and the Ansbachers were asked. Only the Coburgers had declared themselves for Bavaria with a vote in 1919. In the course of the Napoleonic Wars, in which Bavaria took part as an ally of the Corsican, all other parts of Franconia fell to Bavaria, if not better to say they were captured by Bavaria. "Ladies and gentlemen, that was really a radical fissure!" Kern says, appealing for understanding from his listeners. "One moment the seat of an independent ecclesiastical principality, the next only the provinces."

"But," and Kern sounds very convincing now, "in the meanwhile, we feel fine in Bavaria, but, as Franconians, we're concerned not to hide our light under a buschel. Above all, we insist on Bavaria being spelt out as not meaning just

Munich and Old Bavaria." The Franconians are really happy when they manage to rule the whole of Bavaria, which was often the case, including with the help of a Bamberger as prime minister, I mean Dr. Hans Ehard (governed 1946–1950 and 1960–1962). Kern concludes: "Don't worry, there won't be a federal state of Franconia!" The lady from Munich gives Kern a grateful look. She now knows that it would not be a misalliance if she flirted, in moderation, with her Bamberg guide. "I'll show him," she promises herself.

The group leaves the Dominican courtyard. Kern says, one could do a tour just of courtyards in Bamberg. There are so many lovely ones. He wants to show them a few particularly beautiful ones. "But perhaps," he says "we'd have to give them more attractive names, the Dominicans' Patio, for instance." With that remark, he is indirectly emphasizing his view of the name Little Venice, a description that is extremely successful for tourism, but he does not like it.

One of the oldest pharmacies in Germany: the Court Pharmacy in Karolinenstraße

Looking towards the cathedral from the roof of the Old Town Hall

Cathedral Hill – The Culmination of Bamberg's Self-image

Their path now takes them to the cathedral, even though their route cannot be described as the direct one. But Kern puts the greatest value on it, because, as he says, it gets you in the mood for the cathedral. It is not at all easy to find out how to approach a cathedral in the right manner. Most tourists climb up Karolinenstraße or up the flight of steps on Katzenberg hill to the cathedral – that is if they even manage to tear themselves away from the fascination of the temple of smoked beer, Schlenkerla, where many a visitor gets stuck, without even setting eyes on the cathedral.

Opposite Schlenkerla, Kern's group enters the narrow alley named Ringleinsgasse. Where it ends in Karolinenstraße, there are two interesting houses: on the left the Marshalk von Ostheim House with a lovely stairwell, the work of one of the Dientzenhofers. Unfortunately it is not open to the public. On the right is the Court Pharmacy,

one of the oldest pharmacies in Germany. A white Baroque Holy Trinity group, carved by Georg Reuß, shines from the sandstone façade. If you want to see the Baroque fittings of the pharmacy, you will have to go to Heidelberg. They are in the German Pharmacy Museum up in the castle. The herb room, dating from the Rococo Era, is still here.

The group passes the Court Pharmacy and walks on up the cathedral hill, but, a few metres farther on, they turn left into Roppeltsgasse and from there into the street called Vorderer Bach. Everything before their eyes seems to turn yellow. Two houses, standing next to each other, the pretty "Barockhotel am Dom" and the neighbouring Old Ebrach Court, the Bamberg town house of the Cistercians in Ebrach, were painted in this bright yellow after restoration. Traces of the original paint that were found decided the colour.

Staircase in Marschalk von Ostheim House

Kern thinks, that, in spite of the very frequent use of yellow, there is no cause to feel threatened by a yellow danger. Yellow goes with Baroque. In the 18th century there were even incentives to inspire people to use it as often as possible and put it on their façades. But it was put on a bit thick here in Vorderer Bach.

Kern invites them to look at one of the two "yellow" houses, the "Barockhotel", from the inside. He would like to show them one tiny detail. He thinks that it is important, in that it makes clear to the beholder, that everything in Bamberg has its own special history. The detail is a putto as ornamentation on the Baroque staircase that leads to the first floor. Kern specifically points out that he has a gun barrel at his feet. Why exactly a gun barrel? Kern says this is a reference to the builder of the house, one of the Aufsees family, local nobility. He was the bishop's cupbearer and commander of the ecclesiastical principality's artillery, hence the gun barrel. The group likes such stories and they all laugh.

But Kern is already urging them on up the steep flight of steps that lead out of Vorderer Bach. At the same time, he draws attention to the fact that flights of steps are the "joints" of the Old Town. The topography of the seven hills and the valleys between them creates such extreme conditions that it would not have been possible to master the differences in terrain without the aid of steps. So steps wherever you look: here in Vorderer Bach, an even steeper flight from Hinterer Bach up to the Kaulberg hill, from Katzenberg to the cathedral square, from the street called Sutte to Maternstraße, from the fountain, "Grünhundsbrunnen", up to Ottoplatz, from Sandstraße to Maienbrunnen, from the street up St. Stephen's Hill to "Maria Hilf", from Leinritt to Alter Graben and not to forget the one that leads from Eisgrube to Frauenplatz, meaning "women's square" or, right next to it, to Hölle, the street called "Hell".

At the top of the steps, Kern makes them stop. "Just look at the view!" he says with a note of enthusiasm. Their eyes wander from the Renaissance gable of the Old Ebrach Court in the foreground, over the Baroque of the New Ebrach Court behind and then across to the Gothic of the Upper Parish Church, "like the backdrops of the town as a stage", as Kern describes the juxtaposition of styles. He will shortly be showing them another example, the fourth. The group walks the few steps along the little street that leads to the cathedral square. They pass the chapterhouse with the Diocesan Museum and find themselves standing in front of the east chancel of the cathedral. Kern asks the group to stop there for a few minutes. At this spot he just has to give a little talk.

"Ladies and gentlemen," he begins, his tone a little too solemn, "we're now approaching the climax of our tour of the city, the cathedral. It is an imperial cathedral, not just the cathedral of the people. You've probably got that feeling already. That it's a building ennobled through and through, that doesn't humble itself to anyone, on the contrary, it gives you the impression, especially here by the east chancel, that it's a castle and you have to knock at the gate to be allowed in." You have to study it long enough for the harmony, which is a mark of the building, to reveal itself to you. Although it was built on the threshold of a decisive change in style, from Romanesque to Gothic, the cathedral still seems a unified whole. To be sure at this end, the older east chancel, it radiates the great calm of Romanesque architecture, the ordered relationship in proportions between weight and support. Towards the west end, culminating in the two west towers, the stone takes on more life, more free interplay. Early Gothic, coming across the Rhine from France, allows the stonework to develop, structures it and breaks up the lines, removes its blocklike appearance, the "stonelike", ornaments it and makes it into ornamentation in itself.

Kern senses he must restrain himself. So he takes refuge in a more reserved and sober tone, that of the recitation of dates, and wants to give them a very brief outline of Bamberg's history, here in front of the cathedral. He is simply unable to avoiding doing this. After all, he is responsible that they all understand the role Bamberg played. And Kern tells them: "Here, on this hill, the cathedral hill, a fortress once stood – the fortress of the Babenbergers. This noble family was engaged in a quarrel with the Konradiners in Würzburg. The reason for the dispute: predominance in East Franconia, which both sides wanted to exercise. We possess a rather accurate witness to this in the

View of the cathedral in wintery twilight

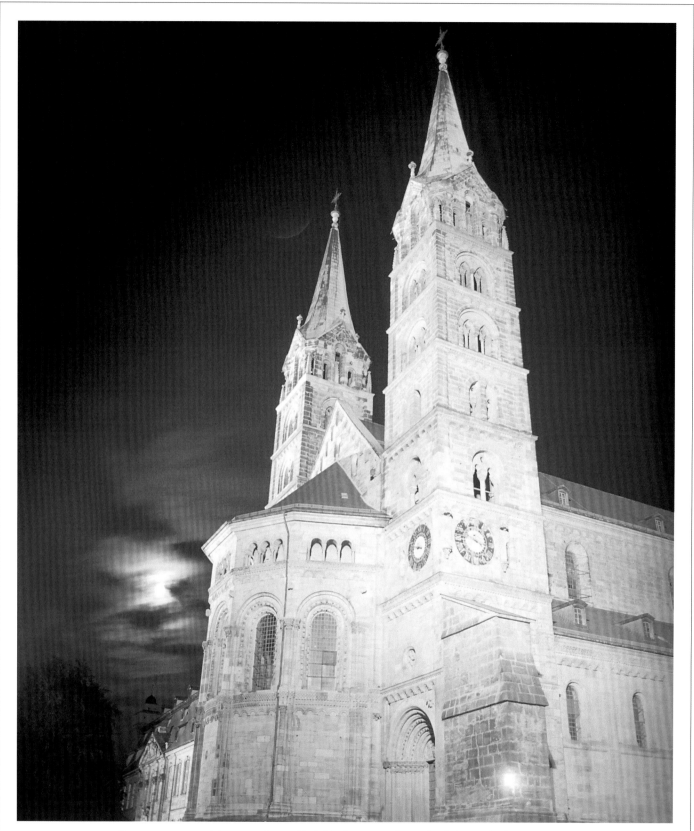

Romanesque architecture in artificial light: east chancel of the cathedral by night

Winter night by the Lady Portal

chronicle of Regino von Prüm, who made an exact record, for the year 902, of the so-called Babenberger Feud and, in particular, of the catastrophe in which it ends for the Babenbergers. At the end, the last of the Babenberger line, Adalbert, is beheaded at Theres, a place between Haßfurt and Schweinfurt. His fortress falls into possession of the crown.

Seventy years later, in 973, King Otto II gives the Babenberger fortress, which in the meantime had been "used" as an imperial prison for the Lombard king, Berengar, and his wife, to the Duke of Bavaria, "Henry the Quarrelsome". He in turn leaves it to his son, Henry, later to be Emperor Henry II. Henry is elected German king in the year 1002 and gives the fortress to his wife, Kunigunde, from the House of Lützelburg (Luxembourg) as her "morning gift".

The "morning gift" was a present, generally property and land, given to the bride by her husband the morning after the wedding. From his youth, Henry must have had a very affectionate attachment to the Babenberger fortress. Five years later he makes it the seat and centre of a bishopric which he begged to be allowed to found at the imperial synod in Frankfurt. Thus Bamberg enters its place in history.

Kern goes on to report that Henry endowed and furnished this, "his" Bamberg so richly, that historical research concludes that such a passion for endowments could not possibly have been just for the capital of a border bishopric and a small ecclesiastical feudal state. The king and emperor must have had more in mind with Bamberg. Presumably he wanted to give the Holy Roman Empire its grievously lacking capital with Bamberg. It is only with this "Bamberg Idea" that various consequences can be explained. Firstly Bamberg was given possessions scattered all over the whole of South Germany and Austria, stretching right down to Carinthia. Then the palace of the emperor and bishop was built right next to the first cathedral, which Henry had built. Henry's chancellor was made first bishop of Bamberg. Furthermore Henry furnished his foundation with book treasures, made it a city of books, and with a school, or what would now be called a university, in which the elite of the empire was to be educated. Finally he gave "his" Bamberg the holy relics, from which mystic power has radiated, even in fact right up to the present day, the charisma of a metropolis.

To end his crash course in Bamberg's history, Kern says Bamberg's innate role is most clearly

"Cathedral toad" next to the Lady Portal

Tympanum of the Lady Portal

Slab covering the Imperial Tomb

Side panel of the Lady Altar

explained by an event of world importance at Easter 1020. Pope Benedict VIII travelled over the Alps to Bamberg to discuss all the relevant matters of the world with Henry. A summit conference shortly after the first millennium.

Kern thinks that all this, Bamberg's role in history, as well as the beginnings of the city that was literally catapulted into history, can be sensed nowhere better than in the place where they want to go next anyway – in the cathedral. This cathedral is in fact the third one, the one finished in 1237. The two preceding buildings fell victim to fire. But the third cathedral follows the tradition of the "founding era". Above all two tombs inside add additional honour. In any case, says Kern, he will be making some remarks about them later, when they are standing right by the tombs.

The group goes up the few steps to the so-called cathedral terrace, from where the holy relics of the cathedral treasure used to be shown to the deeply moved throng of pilgrims – a periodic spectacle in the history of the town. On the way to the Lady Portal they pass one of the "cathedral toads", by which two sculptures of lions are meant, that guard the two entrances to the east

chancel, Adam's and Lady Portal. Erosion and mechanical wear and tear by children riding on them have changed their appearance so much, that now they do indeed look more like toads than regular lions.

Kern, obviously trying again and again to liven up his tour of the city with stories, tells them about one of the most recent "Bamberg miracles". It concerns Heiner Bosch, who died some years ago. He was chairman of the townspeople's association for the district the cathedral stands in. A master craftsman by trade and town councillor, he was an ardent smoker of cigars. So he always used to light one of his beloved cigars on his way to the cathedral on Sunday, even though it was only such a short way. When he reached the cathedral, he did not want to throw it away – craftsmen are always thrifty people in their heart of hearts – because he had only smoked the tip. Consequently the district chairman stubbed out his cigar in the "nostril" of a cathedral toad and deposited it there until he came out from his Sunday duties. Then he would light it again and finish it with obvious enjoyment. And now the miracle: one day, when Bosch returned an hour later after taking part in

Mass and Eucharist and reached for his cigar, it was, as expected, still sticking out of the cathedral toad's nostril. But when he lit it, the cigar smoker was almost startled by the discovery that the cigar had turned into an untouched, fresh from the shop and equally agreeably smelling cigar. To this day nobody, except for the "miracle worker", knows who it was who removed the butt and replaced it with a cigar from his own box.

"A lovely story," says the lady from Munich with a caressing look as soft as velvet for Kern. This confuses Kern so much that he gives the wrong ratio between the "Bamberg foot" and "Bamberg cubit". He corrects himself, it is two to five. The bronze marks to the right of the Lady Portal demonstrate the two measurements. Now they finally enter the cathedral by that door and Kern begins to speak very softly. He says the cathedral is not a museum. It is cathedral and parish church in one. Unfortunately many visitors disregard that and behave accordingly. He is going to speak softly and asks them to understand why. They all nod. Kern has already told his group outside that, inside the cathedral, the atmosphere pervading at the time of founding has been preserved. That is not entirely true, for, as in other churches, the original impression of the interior has been changed and partly covered over by numerous additional fixtures and furnishings in the following centuries, mainly in the Baroque Era, not surprisingly.

Under the Bavarian king, Ludwig I, a ruler definitely appreciative of art and who the state owes much to, almost all these additions, regardless of their artistic rank, were literally swept out of the cathedral, if not to say thrown out. Such a cleansing of style is called purification. Kern: "You can regard this as a mortal sin against the spirit of protection of historical monuments or as an attempt to restore the original state. My opinion lies between the two. I can understand Ludwig's motives, but I condemn the thoughtlessness with which they were carried out." However, the cathedral now has a pronounced simplicity, an almost elitist plainness. Yet just because of that, the works of art from the "initial furnishing" and some objects of later date, that have been left, come almost obtrusively to splendid effect. Kern cannot help, in view of this, adding the remark

that it is superfluous to go into detail over the for and against of installing stained glass windows, as the cathedral chapter has contemplated.

Kern next shows them the Visitation Group on the north parclose of the east chancel with the figures of Elizabeth, Mary, the Laughing Angel and St. Denis, who is carrying his head under his arm, as well as the effigy from the slab of Pope Clement II's tomb. Personally, says Kern, he feels the figure of Elizabeth is the best one. The face of a seeress! Elizabeth knows that Mary will be the mother of the Son of God. Her look proclaims this.

A few steps on and the group is standing under the Rider. Kern leads his people to a spot from where they can look up at the best known work of art in the cathedral at an angle. In secret, he is glad that not one of them remarks in disappointment: "I imagined him bigger!" As if one can measure art of this class in metres or kilos...

Bamberg Rider

Monument to Bishop von Hohenlohe

St. John, a figure on the altar made by Glesker

St. Elizabeth from the Visitation group

Relief in the row of Prophets

A mediaeval masterpiece: the statue of Synagogue

No, the Rider is large enough for this group! "We don't know much about the Rider," says Kern, "not who made him, which is understandable, for the mediaeval artist often remains anonymous, comes second to his work. Nor do we know with absolute certainty who the Rider portrays. The attempts to interpret his identity would fill a whole bookshelf." The most probable assumption, consolidated by recent research, is that it is Emperor Henry's brother-in-law, St. Stephen, king of Hungary.

For many people, the version that one can see King Philip of Swabia in the Rider seems more plausible. In 1208, he was murdered by Otto von Wittelsbach not very far from this spot, over in the Old Court. Kern adds that Walther von der Vogelweide described Philip as daring and handsome, as the "best of all Hohenstaufers" – and the Bamberger Rider is certainly a good-looking man, too. Besides, one fact in favour of the Philip theory is that the murdered king was initially buried in the Bamberg cathedral, exactly opposite the pillar on which the figure now stands. Later he was exhumed and found his last resting-place in the royal burial vault in the cathedral in Speyer. But, if the Rider was really Philip, would Bishop Ekbert, the builder of the cathedral, have set up a monument to the very person in whose death he was supposed to have been involved? In fact, this accusation was later proved to have been false.

Still, links between the violent death of Philip of Swabia and the figure of the horseman could still be made in that Bishop Ekbert, just because of the accusations that he was embroiled in the regicide as an accessory, was outlawed. He therefore fled to his sister in Hungary. She was married to the Hungarian king, Andrew. Perhaps, says Kern, he recognized there what an outstanding figure St. Stephen was and set up a monument to him later, once the outlawry was lifted and he returned to Bamberg. Kern brings his digression to an end: "Whoever he is, let's regard him as a symbolic

Well in the crypt under the east chancel

Adam and Eve from Adam's Portal

Choir stalls in the east chancel

The Holy Nail relic in the Holy Nail Chapel

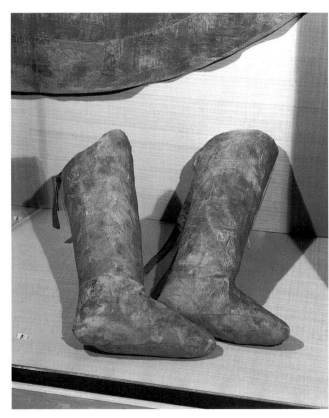

Fabrics from the pope' tomb (Diocesan Museum)

figure of the Christian king! That is surely not a misinterpretation of the Rider." But, above all, we should not claim him just for ourselves as a national symbol, as happened in the Third Reich, we should not make him into a super German. The Occident was more European-minded than we Germans today, on the threshold of a new, mainly seen as an economic Europe in our age, are ready to accept.

Kern now leads his group on to the Imperial Tomb, created by Tilman Riemenschneider from Würzburg. Carved in Franconian marble, it was made from 1499 to 1513. It is a "real tomb" where the mortal remains of the emperor, St. Henry, and the empress, Kunigunde, made a saint likewise, really do lie. This is known because of the repeated relocation of the tomb until it was moved to its present (and hopefully final) place in front of the east choir. Kern: "Wherever the tomb stands and has stood in the past, it marks the centre of the bishopric and is the destination of perpetual pilgrimage to the founders of the bishopric, for whom worship has not waned, even though there has been so much niggling about the two."

Kern explains the reliefs on the tomb – pure picture stories, pious comics with scenes from the lives of the two saints. Kern, himself, likes the story about the curing of the emperor, from the infliction of a stone, by St. Benedict in the monastery of Monte Cassino. According to the legend, while the emperor slept, Benedict removed a painful bladder and kidney stone, a stone as large as a boy's hand, in an operation which caused no bleeding.

"A second king, namely Konrad III, the first Hohenstaufen, lies buried down there," says Kern and asks his group to look through the lovely carved aperture down into the crypt under the east chancel, a Romanesque undercroft of great dignity. He was present when that tomb was moved, too, in the 1970's, says Kern. "When the little casket with the remains of the king was lifted out of the tomb, all the witnesses of the event sensed something that one otherwise feels only in the form of a metaphor, the proverbial 'breath of history'."

Kern's group walks up the main aisle of the cathedral, the last part of the via triumphalis, which was mentioned before down in the town,

Pope's tomb in St. Peter's Choir

Princes' Portal with the Last Judgment

to the main altar on the steps leading to the west choir. It is a modern work by Klaus Backmund from Munich – the lady from Munich reacts at once: "At last!" she says. The Glesker altar, an early-Baroque work, towers up, shining gold, in front of the apsis of the choir. Here, in the west chancel, is the papal tomb, the only one north of the Alps. The group can only look at it from a distance, for the west chancel is closed to visitors, a measure Kern asks them to understand. If people were allowed to go there unhindered, with certainty many a small piece of the choir stalls, perhaps the thick plait of the Queen of Sheba there on the wing of the stall, would be broken off and taken off as a souvenir. From bitter experience, one has to assume that such behaviour can occur. The choir stalls date from the late 14th century. The artists who carved them can be attributed to the Parler circle from Prague.

Kern goes on to talk about the pope's tomb. Pope Clement II lies buried in it. In 1046, as Bishop Suidger of Bamberg, he was called to the See of Rome. But, even though Holy Father, he wanted to be buried where his love lay: in Bamberg that, in his own words, he was as close to as "a bridegroom to his bride". Clement died near the town of Pesaro on the Adria, while on a visitation journey in 1047. He was initially buried there, later brought home over the Alps. You can see the vestments he was buried in in the Diocesan Museum adjoining the cathedral.

Kern then makes a fundamental summary of the facts. In the Bamberg cathedral, he says, pope and emperor lay opposite each other, figures of the two powers that so often quarrelled and were at war with each other, but were just as often united and allies in their caring charge of the Kingdom on Earth and the Kingdom of Heaven. The

Visitors in front of the Princes' Portal with the New Residence behind

Corpus Christi procession in front of the cathedral

Corpus Christi procession in front of the Old Court

cathedral is a part of this great order of things. Kern makes a long pause before, in a soft voice, he asks his group to move on past the monument to Bishop Hohenlohe, which he explains briefly, and on to the Christmas Altar, the work of Veit Stoß, in the south aisle. Kern informs them that the altar reached Bamberg and the cathedral in a roundabout way. It was intended for the Nuremberg Carmelite Monastery but could not be installed there, because, by the time it was finished, Nuremberg had been reformed. So now it is possible to see works by the two great carvers of late-mediaeval art in Germany, works by Veit Stoß and Tilman Riemenschneider, and compare them – and that in the cathedral, something that is not possible anywhere else, as far as he knows, except in museums.

Before the group leaves the cathedral, where he could spend hours showing them more, Kern leads them to a last stop, to the figures on the south parclose of the east chancel – to Synagogue and Ecclesia, embodiments of the Old and New Testaments. As a pair, they are an attempt to link the two together, one of the great themes of mediaeval art. Kern makes no secret of the fact that

the figure of Synagogue has a special fascination for him. The figure, he says, in a bold comparison, is moving so regally, as if she had learnt it in a school for models. As he says it, Kern involuntarily pulls back his shoulders, takes on the contrapposto, that is he puts his weight on his pivot leg and lets his free leg circle freely. And he asks his group to regard how finely the unknown artist has worked the flow of the gown – a brilliant achievement! But now he must allow himself a superlative, namely: "The great figures of the Bamberg cathedral belong to the most mature achievements in mediaeval sculpture." Nobody contradicts him. The lady from Munich tries the contrapposto, draws back her shoulders, pushes her hip forward. Not at all bad, thinks Kern, but is of the opinion Synagogue can do it (even) better.

Back in the cathedral square, Kern draws attention to its beauty, even though it is a conglomeration of different styles: the Romanesque and Gothic of the cathedral, the Renaissance of the Old Court and the Baroque of the prince bishops' New Residence. Since the middle of the 1980s, the square has not been used as a car park any more, on account of its dignified rank and for

Bearers of the guild maces in the Corpus Christi procession

New Residence seen from the cathedral terrace

New Residence seen from the roof of the cathedral

Memorial plaque to Berthier (wall of the New Residence)

the protection of its buildings and works of art. Unfortunately there is still nothing anyone can do about the destruction of the sandstone through exhaust fumes. Anyone who parks his car (except on Sunday morning for church) must reckon with a severe fine. The Bamberg traffic wardens know no mercy.

"Talking about penance," says Kern, "let's go over to the Princes' Portal of the cathedral first. That'll certainly make you feel more penitent." The splendid entrance is only opened on high feast days. On either side, the Apostles stand on the shoulders of the Prophets. The figures are, of course, replicas cast in stone, because the originals have been removed from exposure to the aggressive effects of the weather and are now in the Diocesan Museum, in the cathedral cloisters. The Prophets and Apostles recall the same theme, Old and New Testaments, as Synagogue and Ecclesia, but this time in a male version, so to speak. To Kern it is more important to interpret the Last Judgment in the tympanum – another picture story, moreover the "really most final one there can be, about life after death". Kern draws their attention to the fact that on the side of the damned,

to the left of the Judge of the World, there is also a king, a bishop and even a pope, clearly indicated by crown, mitre and zucchetto. The Devil himself has already enchained them and is just about to drag them down into the realm of eternal darkness. Kern: "We so often accuse the Middle Ages of being a time of bondage and restriction, in which people and their thinking were held, and thereby overlook how free this age was, too. They were so free that they could, for example, perfectly well imagine and express it publicly through art on the portal of a cathedral, that pope, king and bishop will face judgment one day, too." Kern asks his listeners to take an exact look at the smiles the unknown master has written all over their faces. They range from the smile of the simple-minded and the smile of the blessed right to the shrill, bizarre, grimacing laughter on the "other" side. "Let's go!" says Kern – and is quiet all the way over to the entrance of the New Residence. There is no judgment there.

Under the rule of Prince Bishop Lothar Franz von Schönborn, the New Residence was erected by Leonhard Dientzenhofer from 1697 to 1703. All Kern says is that the Baroque prince bishops lived there – until secularization. Since then their successors, no longer sovereign rulers, but "only" bishops, though archbishops, have had to live more modestly, further up the hill in a palais in Obere Karolinenstraße. Kern says they will pass it later on. After the dissolution of the ecclesiastical principality of Bamberg, the kingdom and later the Free State of Bavaria had in fact tried to leave the mighty secular building a real touch of residence, for instance by lodging royals there. By this Kern means the five years from 1862 to 1867, when King Otto of Greece, second son of the Bavarian king, Ludwig I, that is son of the "purifier of the cathedral", took Bamberg and its former residence as his seat in exile. This was after "his" Greek people had driven him out after a good 30 years of rule. Real power, says Kern, focused only once more on the New Residence in the year 1919, when the government of the Free State of Bavaria had to clear out of Munich to escape the soviet republic which had been proclaimed there and got out to Bamberg, where they took up quarters in the Residence. Now the building houses only an Old German Gallery and the former apartments of

Wall and ceiling frescoes in the Emperor's Chamber in the prince bishop's residence

Reception room in the New Residence (before renovation)

the prince bishops, which you can visit, which he very much recommends. There are also rooms for exhibitions and the Bamberg State Library, which is the main occupant. It looks after the book treasures that were bestowed on Bamberg scarcely had it taken its place in history.

In the Emperor's Chamber on the second floor, anniversaries can be celebrated, receptions held and concerts performed. The town and its guests make so much use of it that the Bavarian Office for Palaces, Lakes and Parks, which is in charge of it, speaks more of overusage rather than the Residence having fallen into a Sleeping Beauty existence.

From Sleeping Beauty it is not difficult for Kern to lead on to the Rose Garden that they are going to next. "You've seen so many old stones in the last few hours and have walked so long on old cobblestones that you have a right just to feel the ground under your feet for a while," he says and leads his group right, from the paved inner courtyard of the Residence through a small gate

Rose Garden with St. Michael's in the background

Rose Garden seen from above

in the wall. He waits until the last one has passed through. It is clear from the expression on his face that Kern is very much looking forward to the surprise he can offer them by visiting the Rose Garden.

It leaves not one of the eleven women and men unimpressed. Nobody can hold back, they all want to express their delight. "Beautiful, fantastic, quite unique," are the first comments. The lady from Munich, a relatively young woman of almost forty, makes her comment fashionably short. "Super!" she says. And breaths the scent of the roses into her dainty nose.

The Rose Garden of the New Residence harmonizes two conflicting yearnings of the human race: first it answers the primeval longing for security, for being protected, for home. This basic feeling is conveyed by the fact, immediately obvious to every visitor, that around 5,000 roses can flower and give off their fragrance in lavish

splendour, protected, and in the lee of the wind, by high buildings, that lay their arms round the garden. Since the residence buildings form a trapezium, the fourth side open to the Rose Garden, the east side of the garden is like the apron of a stage opening to the "stalls", that is to the open landscape. Our eyes rove over the brick red and slate black roofs of the town across to the Jura hills, to Giechburg Castle and Gügel Church, to the rounded hilltops by Ludwag and the craggy edge of the Jura above Würgau, to the "blue hills". A scene that inspires our imagination, lures us out of ourselves.

Kern utters further thoughts: "These are exactly the feelings that keep our continual travels on the go, the irresistible urge to go out into the outside world and the sheer joy afterwards of being able to be home again. In the framework of this interplay lies the Rose Garden, grows, flowers and flourishes!"

Looking through the gateway of the Old Court to the New Residence

The inner courtyard of the Old Court

Every summer: Calderón Festival in the Old Court

Kern and his group are in the best of moods. There is a pleasant fragrance in the air, the statues on their sandstone socles have a mischievous expression on their faces and – in so far as the figures are female – "ample bosoms", as Kern remarks and tries to catch the eye of the pretty lady from Munich. Beyond the garden, on the hill on the other side of Austraße, the former Benedictine monastery of St. Michael's towers up; in the left corner is a delightful tiny building, a Rococo stone pavilion. Involuntarily one calls hoop skirts and wigs, powder and minuet to mind, feels a wish for music and someone to take by the hand and stroll gracefully between the flowering rosebeds: one-two, one-two, ta-ta-taa...

By the pavilion, which is run as a café, there is a smell of freshly made coffee. But Kern does not allow them a coffee break. "Please, content yourselves with the scent of the roses," he says and stops all protests. "Cad!" says the lady from Munich, but trots obediently behind him and out of the Rose Garden.

The group takes a rather anachronic route from the New Residence to the Old Court, from Baroque to Renaissance and late-Gothic. Kern stops by the lovely gateway to the Old Court. He asks his people, whether they can think who the long-haired layabout – yes, he really uses this long outdated expression – and the full-bosomed lady on the stone crossbeam could represent. The group puzzles over the question, but finds no answer. Kern solves the puzzle: "They are allegories for the two most important rivers in the Bamberg bishopric, on the left the Main, on the right the Regnitz. A foot is missing on the 'Main', 'Regnitz' is letting a little angel tickle hers."

The inner courtyard of the Old Court fills them with the same delight, as they had felt just before in the Rose Garden. But it is enclosed on all sides. With the exception of the Council Chamber in the building facing the cathedral square, which was built in the Renaissance Era, late-Gothic half-timbering is the dominant feature with high, steep roofs, intercepted by rows of dormer windows

"Foot Tickler" on the Beautiful Gate of the Old Court

"Bamberg Idols" in the History Museum

under tiny long slanting roofs. The warm, dark wood of the long galleries, their parapets brightly coloured with geraniums and petunias, is another striking feature. Kern tells them the flats behind the galleries were not vacated until a few decades ago – out of fear that continued use of the Old Court held too many risks for the old buildings. The experience in the devastating fire in Trausnitz castle above Landshut played a role in this decision. The whole complex of the Old Court is being turned into a museum, as is already the case in the Renaissance part, where the History Museum of the City of Bamberg is housed. While the Diocesan Museum in the chapterhouse next to the cathedral is an attempt to depict the importance and splendour of the former ecclesiastical principality, the History Museum concerns itself with the role the townspeople played in their town's art and history.

Standing in the middle of the inner courtyard, Kern says that the annual Calderón Festival takes place there every July. After some years, they got away from the idea of performing only works by the Spanish Baroque poet. Always just Calderón would have been too much pathos, too much entanglement in sin and guilt, ideas many people can no longer understand. But still, Calderón's dramas, such as "La Vida es Sueño" or "The Judge of Zalamea" were great successes in the Old Court open-air theatre.

As far as the one-time importance of the court immediately after the founding of the bishopric of Bamberg and in the following two, three centuries is concerned, Kern has a comparison which seems abstruse at first. He talks about a "mediaeval chancellor's bungalow with a steep roof" (in reference to the famous bungalow built for the German chancellors in Bonn), about a centre of power, where the administration of the empire had its seat, at least at times, and from where the affairs of the empire were conducted. The Imperial Chamber of Henry's day still exists, if only in fragments.

To finish, Kern brings in further marginalia relating to the use of the whole complex for solely museum purposes. Basically, he describes this as right, but his personal opinion is that it would become the buildings and the town, if there was a break in one or two places with a "somewhat

Spiral staircase in the History Museum

Bay and relief on house No. 9 Domstraße

more lively use". He is thinking of an artist's studio for example, where visitors to the court could have a look in, or even a "museum inn". In any case, that loud hammering is to be heard from over there in the northwest wing leaves a refreshing impression on him and many visitors. It reminds one that the cathedral stonemasons are housed there. Bamberg really must avoid being compared to a museum, he concludes his chain of thought – and not even to a museum of urban architecture.

The group leaves the courtyard by the gateway opposite the "Beautiful Gate". It leads into Domstraße. Kern wants to show them two of the lovely courtyards which he had enthused about down in the town. The first one is the courtyard of the cathedral provost's offices, No. 5 Domstraße, with a quite unique view of the west towers of the cathedral through the branches of a sweet chestnut. The second one is the neighbouring Meranier Court, No. 7 Domstraße, its quiet protected by three gates and a high wall with a battlement parapet. The group expresses its pleasure that they are getting to know Bamberg "in-depth", too. A look inside buildings and courtyards gives an even truer picture of the town. In response Kern remembers a quotation by Karl Immermann (1837). According to him, Bamberg is a town full of rare objects, like an old grandmother's chest of drawers, in which she has collected a lot of things. "Then let's enjoy rummaging about, we're sure to find a few more lovely rarities!"

Kern and his group continue on up Domstraße, past the curacy houses built in the 1920s, past the lovely Madler Court and the coats of arms on the walls. Domstraße ends in Obere Karolinenstraße by the part that widens into a square. Two sprawling courts – Buseck Court, No. 6, and Langheimer Court, No. 8, (once the town residence of the Cistercians of Langheim Monastery near Lichtenfels, the second most important Cistercian monastery in the bishopric after Ebrach) – as well as the magnificent view of the "broadside" of St. Michael's Monastery, which opens up between the two, are the features of the north side of the square. The south wall is formed by the palais, erected to designs by Michael Küchel in the second half of the 18th century. Since secularization it has served as archbishop's palace. Its façade heralds in a new style: early Classicism.

Archbishop's Palace

Romanesque nave of St. James's Church (before renovation)

Farther up the hill, past the diagonally located mission house of St. Henry, a palais of about the same period as the Archbishop's Palace, the street narrows to the spot where there used to be a gateway into the cathedral close. It is so narrow that drivers and pedestrians alike have to be careful not to get caught between the uphill and downhill traffic. The group walks through to the square beyond, Jakobsplatz. In spite of their slow pace and without Kern pointing it out, they sense the feeling of a continuous change from expanse to narrowness, from a bottleneck to space. It is so typical of Bamberg's Old Town and literally hits you in the eye here.

Kern thinks Jakobsplatz is certainly something to be proud of, too. It lies on the spur of a hill. The land falls almost startlingly steep to the left and the right. On the left there is a view of open countryside stretching right up to Altenburg Castle. On the right the church on the Michelsberg hill looks down on the scene below it. Lovely, well-proportioned houses of the nobility frame the square, but the dominant feature is Jakobskirche, St. James's Church, one of the oldest churches in Bamberg. It was consecrated in 1109, though the beholder will find this hard to believe when he first sees it. St. James's seems considerably younger. As is usual in Bamberg, the church, a Romanesque building, was "made to have" a Baroque façade during the Baroque Age. The result was so successful that nobody has had cause for complaint, not even to the present day.

A larger-than-life statue of St. James the Younger stands in a niche below the gable; the great Baroque sculptor, Ferdinand Tietz, created it: a large figure of a man, striding out with verve, with traveller's hat and staff. Kern recalls the great mediaeval pilgrimage to Santiago de Compostela in Northern Spain, to the grave of St. James found there. Bamberg's St. James's Church was a stage on the Way of St. James to the greatest destination in Christianity for pilgrims – after Jerusalem and Rome. It was busily frequented all through the Middle Ages and has regained its relevance in recent times. The Way of St. James coming from Bohemia and the one from Thuringia met here, joined into one and led on to Frankfurt.

Jakob Kern – at this point we really must mention Kern's Christian name again – invites them into the church for a short visit. "Just sit in the pews and take in the Romanesque effect of the interior, especially the feeling of rhythm emanating from the pillars and arches," he advises. The pillars rest on massive bases and end in mighty cushion capitals. The two rows lend the interior great solemnity. "The church reminds me of Alpirsbach in the Black Forest," one of them says. Kern just nods. It is quiet in St. James's. Only few tourists find their way here. Most visitors carry out their "duty visit to the cathedral" and leave it at that. A pity.

Head of statue of St. James on St. James's Church

In the courtyard of Langheimer Court

Station of the Cross in Aufseßstraße

St. James's Church seems abandoned for a further reason, too: until a few years ago, the Franciscans in the Franciscan monastery opposite were in charge of it. Now the monastery is closed, has "dried up" like all the others, except for the Carmelite one, that they will visit later. For a time, children of emigrants of German origin from Eastern Europe learned the language of their fathers, or rather their grandfathers – a closed book for them until then – in the former Franciscan monastery. Kern gives them the signal to set off again.

Their walk round the town is about to turn into more of a hike, but only a short one, he says. He is sure it will do them all good to step it out a bit. To begin with, the group goes down the steep slope of the street leading to Michelsberg. At the place where the Franziskanergässchen, a lane cascading down like a mountain stream from the left, ends, Kern turns right into Aufseßstraße; it descends gently back down to the town. On the right is the high wall of the cathedral precincts, a reminder of the former fortress, while on the left there is a school boarding house, the Aufseesianum, built in the 18th century. On the wall of its large garden there are three stations of the Cross. The way of the Cross begins at St. Elizabeth's Church in the Sand District and stretches up to

St. Michael's by night

St. Faith's, the former provost's church of the Michelsberg monastery. The scenes depicted on the late-Gothic way of the Cross reveal their close connection with the school of the Nuremberg sculptor, Adam Krafft. About 150 metres farther along the Aufseesianum wall, a gate opens to the left. This is where the path, specially made to lead through the former monastery garden and up to St. Michael's Monastery, begins. The first part is called Benedictine Way, telling us who used to fill the monastery with life and leave their mark on it: monks of the Order of St. Benedict.

The way leads uphill, pretty steep but easy to walk. Every twenty, thirty metres, there is another view, new things to look at. Soon they see a pavilion in the way in the terraced part of the garden. Their path leads them through its lower storey. Kern has another story to tell. One of the last abbots of the monastery – his name is not important – very frequently met the lady of his dreams for a bit of hanky-panky there or in the second pavilion farther on. On account of this liaison the order later transferred him permanently, actually to Rome, for disciplinary reasons. The pavilions however have remained, a reminder of illicit love. "That's the way it goes," figures Kern and then does not know what to say next.

The last part of the way is a flight of steps up to the large Michelsberg terrace. From up there there is a sweeping view of the slate black roofs of the Residence and the cathedral, of the river shining silver and of half the town. From a lookout terrace the visitor can look straight down onto the roofs of the former hospital, today a hotel by the name of "Residenzschloss". It was erected by the public-spirited prince bishop, Franz Ludwig von Erthal, in 1789, the year of the French Revolution. He was a prince of the Church who should have been a ruler exercising the absolute power befitting the age he lived in. In reality he was an enlightened father of his people. The hospital he had built fulfilled its function faithfully and well for almost 200 years, until it was replaced by the town's modern polyclinic.

Kern leads the group along the rear side of the monastery building, past a café and the beer garden of the monastery's inn round the corner. From there you can look out over the silos and cranes of the new harbour and over to the Haß-berge hills and foothills of the Jura in the Upper Main Valley, including the famous hill, Staffelberg, known to many from Victor von Scheffel's song, which begins: "Well now, the air is blowing fresh and pure…"

And then the group enters what must be one of the most beautiful places in the town: the inner courtyard of St. Michael's Monastery. The Mercury fountain, set in the corner of the large well-tended lawn, is edged by bright red geraniums. Geranium red licks over the parapet of the graceful flight of steps leading up to the entrance to the monastery church. Kern tells them, that it is just because of this flight of steps, that Bambergers like to get married in St. Michael's. It gives one an indescribable feeling of stepping out into a new life after the celebration of the marriage service. As well as that, even the biggest wedding party can easily arrange itself for wedding pictures on the wide flight of steps.

The Benedictine monastery of St. Michael belongs to the first endowments bestowed on Bamberg. It was founded at the behest of Henry II in 1015. It has gone through a very varied history, been destroyed – even by an earthquake among other causes – and rebuilt. It possessed a famous writing room, a scriptorium, in which at times up to forty monks were at work. For soon over 200 years the extensive complex has served as an old people's home for the citizens. On festive occasions the town holds equally festive receptions in the former refectory of the monks. The Benedictine "ora et labora" (pray and work), the order's rule, is no longer in effect on the Michelsberg. The people who live here now are resting from their life's work, waiting for their amen. Only prayer is still going on.

The church is basically Gothic but was given a magnificent Baroque façade by Leonhard Dientzenhofer and inside splendid Baroque furnishings, made by the best master craftsmen of the day. As an example, Kern refers to the pulpit. It conveys an effect of almost theatrical motion, an effect that can scarcely be heightened any more. The Devil himself, struck by the word of God and the sword of the archangel, plunges from the soundboard into the depths.

Kern allows his group time to tune into the atmosphere of the church's interior. He shows

Mercury Fountain in the courtyard of St. Michael's Monastery

them the slender choir behind the screen, made of wrought-iron with a wealth of ornamentation, and the massive monuments to the Bamberg prince bishops, made of alabaster and black marble. They were removed from the cathedral during the "purification of style" and set up here. He points up into the Gothic vault, its panels painted with a "Heavenly Garden": a so-called herbarium with around 600 depictions – fairly exact depictions of plants and herbs. Lastly Kern leads his people to the third most important tomb in Bamberg, to the tomb of Bishop Otto the Holy, the third "Bamberg saint". He is also known as the Apostle of the Pomeranians, because he went on two missionary journeys and converted them to Christianity. Otto's tomb is under the raised choir. One can look down on it from above through an aperture in the floor. You can walk, or better expressed, crawl through a narrow passage in the tomb itself.

Whoever forces himself through will be protected from backache in future, says Kern. But, to be on the safe side, he adds that that is a pious promise, commemorating St. Otto. It cannot be verified medically. Nonetheless, the whole group wants to crawl through Otto's tomb. The lady from Munich is last. This means she is alone with Kern for two seconds and has just time to give Kern's hand a squeeze.

Leaving the church, the group enjoys that special feeling you have descending the flight of steps to the monastery courtyard. Incidentally, there is an interesting museum on the right side, the Franconian Brewery Museum. Kern asks for their attention. He says, now is the time to review everything as a whole. He and Bamberg do not have anything more to offer, or rather nothing much lovelier than what he has already shown. But there is something he must convey to his

Tomb of St. Otto in St. Michael's

Holy Sepulchre in St. Michael's

"Heavenly Garden" in St. Michael's

group at all costs: a further example of harmony not mentioned so far, the harmony between the town and the surrounding countryside. To make this more obvious, he suggests going a bit farther up the Michelsberg – not Michaelsberg! He knows somewhere up there where the group can take a rest and have their long deserved coffee or even a glass of wine. A "new dimension" will reveal itself when they look over the rim of their coffee cup or wine glass. The group agrees eagerly, above all because of the promised coffee break. Kern cannot blame them; he well knows that tours of the city like this one are lovely, a rich experience and interesting, but can definitely be quite tiring.

The place Kern was talking about is the Villa Remeis. If it were closed, he had a second café, called "Bergschlösschen", a little higher up "in reserve". On the way they pass the church of St. Faith on the right. Kern says: "We can skip that one, as we've been in four churches already and still have a fifth one ahead of us." If today were Good Friday, then he would insist on visiting St. Faith's. Holy Sepulchres are set up in Bamberg

Church of St. Faith

on Good Friday and one of the most impressive examples is to be found in St. Faith's.

Five minutes later and Kern's people take a seat on the terrace of the Villa Remeis, which is on the left side of St.-Getreu-Straße. They put two tables together to make one big one and order coffee and cake. And enjoy the "review of everything" that this vantage point can offer. Framed by flowers and the branches of the trees that crown the Remeis hill, Bamberg lies below them, like the opened double page of a colourful catalogue of the "dream cities" of the world. The slanting view, through the frame and down the slope, shapes the fall of the folds of the hills and spurs flowing into the valley and likewise the way the town seems to ebb into the countryside. A picture of almost perfect harmony.

Kern has the impression that the members of his group in the face of this "fine picture of a town", are also trying to make their conversation as pleasing as possible. "One talks quite differently from up here," he thinks and no one contradicts him. The lady from Munich has a similar impression. She feels "as if she has wings" and looks at Kern as she says so.

The group is in the best of moods when they continue their walk down the grassy slopes of the Remeis hill, which is covered with fruit trees. Each tree has someone responsible for it, who looks after it and harvests the fruit. Once they reach the built-up area again, Kern tells them they are actually walking on top of nothing but cavities. From here on, the hill is a labyrinth of cellars where the beer from the almost one hundred breweries in the town used to be stored. There are still nine remaining breweries. This system of caverns in the sandstone outcrop begins under the Michelsberg and reaches south to St. Stephen's Hill, where it grows into an unmatched underground world of cellars. "If you come again, I can willingly book you a date for a Bamberg underground tour," says Kern and adds, that exploring the underground tunnels is a real winner in the programme of the municipal adult education centre.

They soon reach St. James's Church, where they leave Jakobsplatz and turn right down the steep descent of Maternstraße. On the left is the wall of the cathedral close, on the right a row of little houses, one of which is still waiting for

Villa Remeis

Countryside and town marry: view from Altenburger Straße

Bamberg in winter seen from Teufelsgraben

Cloisters of the Carmelite Monastery

renovation. Kern says such things are part of the picture: dilapidation made visible. An old town cannot only shine and sparkle, it has to be allowed to crumble and, in moderation of course, rot away. How would you believe its age otherwise? Such a lovely old lady like Bamberg has to powder her face a bit and continually make herself pretty, but she does not need a face-lift. A town's thousand-year-old face needs wrinkles.

At the bottom of the Knöcklein hill, the group has reached the lowest point of this part of their tour. From here they climb up to Karmeliten-platz, where the church and monastery of the Bamberg Carmelites have been for 400 years. Before that the Benedictine Convent of St. Theodore was on the site. Kern leaves out a visit to the church, but points out how old it really is by just showing them the Romanesque zigzag orna-mentation on the walled up portal they pass. To make up, he invites them in to at least a visit to the late-Romanesque cloisters. The brother at the door greets them with a friendly "Grüß Gott" and answers their expected query: "No, it doesn't cost anything to go in."

In the cloisters, Kern tells them that very few Bambergers have had a close look at this "place of quiet". They knew more about the confessionals in the adjoining church, for the Carmelites had the reputation of being especially kind, understand-ing and also tolerant father confessors. "Madam," Kern just cannot stop himself turning to the lady from Munich yet again, "if you needed absolution, which I don't suppose you do, then you'd find it there."

The group walks slowly along the cloisters and Kern refers to the sculptures on the capitals of the pillars – sculpture of the highest quality and to be dated around 1300. But it is not possible for us to work out the meaning of all its symbolism any more. The group thanks the brother at the door and puts some coins into the offertory box, a substitute for no admission charge. Outside the group turns right and a few metres on – there is a fountain on the corner – reach the Kaulberg hill. The street of the same name is the most impor-tant road into the town from the west. The Bam-bergers hope though that people will preferably use the Münchner Ring, the southern ring road, to keep the traffic load on the Old Town as small as

Glassed courtyard of St. Joseph's Home (Jakobsplatz)

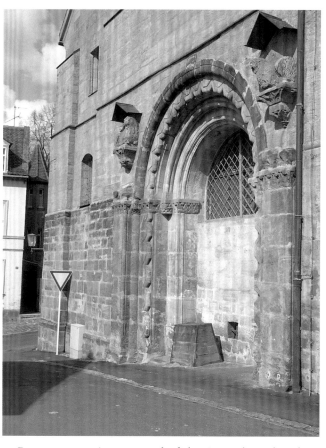

Romanesque zigzag portal of the Carmelite Church

111

Our Gracious Lady

Real doughnuts in the Wedding Feast of Cana crib scene

possible. "But that recommendation doesn't apply to us pedestrians," Kern calls out and asks them to go down the Kaulberg with him and enjoy it. A good hundred yards on, the main Gothic work in the town appears on the right. This is the parish church of Our Lady, called Upper Parish Church for short. It is the most important church in the town for the citizens. Perhaps that is why building was so protracted: nearly a hundred years passed from the laying of the foundation stone in 1338 to completion. As they go down the hill towards it, Kern first draws their attention to the plain west façade and the mighty tower. Instead of a Gothic helm roof as intended, the tower has a boxlike top with a small dome on top. The town lookout used to live in the "box".

The group goes round the church and looks at the 14th-century Wedding Portal with the Wise and Foolish Virgins on the north side. The sheer might of the east chancel fills them with enthusiasm. The Parler family, master builders from Prague, was involved in the building. Kern seizes the opportunity to draw attention to the fact that master builders from Prague, who had trained in Bohemia, enriched and influenced the face of Bamberg in quite considerable measure – above all the Dientzenhofer family. The brilliantly successful Baroquization of Bamberg is owed primarily to them.

The east chancel of the Upper Parish Church can compete with French cathedral Gothic: flying buttresses, pinnacles, filigreely carved stone and an extremely steep roof, soaring clearly up over the ridge of the nave. It seems to divide the heavens like a wedge, when fog lies over the Regnitz Valley and only the chancel of the Upper Parish Church is already free of the mist. Among the many details on the chancel and walls, Kern shows them the tiny "boozer manikin" on a little staircase tower on the south long wall. In reality it is a lookout, who is tooting his horn, a spoonerism on the German word "tütelt", by which the Bambergers, and they are not the only ones, understand habitual drinking.

The main Gothic work in Bamberg has been turned into Baroque inside for the reasons already mentioned several times. You cannot get away from it. Pointed arches were reshaped into round ones, stucco was put on the walls and ceilings.

View from the tower of the Upper Parish Church

Gothic chancel of the Upper Parish Church

The basically Gothic atmosphere survived in the chancel however. The statue of Our Gracious Lady, dating from around 1320, on the high altar, plays an important part in that. The women of Bamberg, in particular, bring their cares to her. Our Gracious Lady is dressed in sumptuous robes on Mary's high feasts. She is taken out of the chancel and placed in front of her congregation in the nave. We have already recorded her meeting with the pietà of St. Martin's.

Kern speaks again with a reference to the fact that the Upper Parish Church has a second great work of art that no one should pass by: a painting by Tintoretto, which shows the Assumption of the Virgin Mary. It was identified and guaranteed to be genuine in a highly unusual restoration process, which took several years. The painting now hangs in the right side aisle, a prime example of the successful conservation of old works and of a high standard in the art of restoration.

"You can't have a more spectacular ascension into Heaven, the start of a loaded rocket into space can't touch it," says Kern. He allows the group time to study Jacopo Tintoretto's large painting, which shines again in its old glory. Jakob Kern, we must name his Christian name a second time after doing so at St. James's Church, tells his group that Bamberg's largest and certainly most interesting crib, a model of the Nativity scene, is set up here in the church during the winter months. After Christmas the scene is changed several times and the one showing the Wedding Feast of Cana with real little sausages and rolls is a delight for crib friends from all over the world.

Kern then motivates his team to undertake one last great effort, the climb up St. Stephen's Hill, the most southerly of the seven hills. The finale of their guided tour will follow shortly afterwards. "Don't worry, we'll hold out to the end," resounds the echo from the group. They descend the steps to Frauenplatz and then more down to the street called Eisgrube, which they follow uphill all the way to St. Stephen's Church. On the way, they go past the house, No. 14, with a strange knob on the door, the so-called "Apple Woman". The Romantic poet, E.T.A. Hoffmann, is supposed to have been inspired by the grotesque face on the knob into creating the scolding market woman in his tale "The Golden Pot". In the tale,

"Assumption of the Virgin Mary" by Tintoretto

Mount of Olives, Upper Parish Church

Light and shade in the street named Eisgrube

The Bamberg "Four Churches View" from St. Stephen's Hill

"Apple Woman" on a door in Eisgrube

Grave of a Romantic writer (St. Stephen's Hill)

she hauls the student, Anselm, over the coals, yelling at him loudly because he pushed against her stall and knocked it over. A few yards farther up the hill, the west façade of St. Stephen's Church – Baroque of course – soars up. Its creator though is not a Neumann nor one of the Dientzenhofers, but Antonio Petrini, who was called over from Würzburg. Kern draws attention to the fact that St. Stephen's Church, or more correctly the preceding building, has an advantage over all the other churches in Bamberg in two different ways: namely it was built at the behest of an empress, St. Kunigunde, and consecrated by a pope, by which Benedict VIII is meant, in 1020. Whoever wants to can perfectly well judge it a sign of the "liberalitas Bavariae" or of the ecumenical movement, that a church consecrated by a pope was handed over to the town's Protestant-Lutherans to become their main church in the 19th century.

Kern walks as far as Stephansplatz with his group. Following the basic Bamberg model for squares, the narrow street widens into a square, only to narrow again at the other end. Kern begs their understanding, if he suggests they should turn left at once and go back down St. Stephen's Hill, instead of mastering the very top of the hill and its beer cellars. The Bambergers call the beer gardens "cellars" because you really are sitting on top of them. He perfectly well knows that it is a sacrilege in Bamberg not to go to them. A visit to a beer cellar would be sure to last so long, for the very reason that it is so pleasant to sit *on* them, that he would find himself unable to finish his walk round the town. The group follows Kern's advice and goes down St. Stephen's Hill with him. Another Bamberg miracle awaits them at the foot: Böttinger House.

Böttinger House is Bamberg's loveliest and, from the point of view of art history, most important secular building. It was the residence of a civil servant at the bishop's court, of the episcopal privy councillor and Franconian legate, Johann Ignaz Michael Tobias Böttinger, who had become rich during the War of the Spanish Succession. He had to secure the supplies to the imperial army and, in so doing, obviously did such good business, that enough was left over for his private coffer. At the beginning of the 18th century, he commissioned Johann Dientzenhofer to erect a

"On" the Greifenklau beer cellar

house for his family at the foot of St. Stephen's Hill. The building site would have deserved the negative rating of "being unsuitable for building" on account of the restricted space available and its steepness. Nowadays one would almost certainly either "shift" it or have the level raised with the help of contractor's machinery. He got a bourgeois palais in which it was not particularly comfortable to live, as later owners were to discover, but a house that – as seen afterwards – is among the best bourgeois secular architecture created in the Baroque Age.

Kern asks his group to stand on the pavement opposite in front of the "House of the Drum", as it is called. From there he shows them the façade first. "This is where your eyes will pop out of your heads," he says drily and adds that almost every detail that was applied to façades in Baroque times can be found here; the floral motifs grow out of the sandstone in tropical abundance and grow rampantly over the eaves and right up onto the roof. In answer to the group's question as to why

the house is painted in one single colour, Kern says: "That's just the way it is!" According to the curators of monuments, the façade was already so "enlivened" by plastic art, that they could not recommend further emphasis of the details with an extra colour. In any case, they had reckoned the patina would, in time, take on different shades naturally – and it had worked out that way. The uniform plain ochre had shown a different texture in a few years.

The group goes through the acanthus-framed portal to the courtyard – an exception, as unfortunately Böttinger House can be viewed only from outside. The garden rises in terraces at the back. Now it becomes clear: Dientzenhofer, in a moment of inspiration, turned an adverse location into the basis for a palace built specially for a steep slope. Each floor opens onto a terrace of corresponding height.

Kern asks his group to turn round and look at the side of the courtyard behind them. Astonishment. The original façade in the centre of the

Baroque interior: stairwell in Böttinger House

Ornamentation beyond all measure: portal of Böttinger House

three wings is obviously missing. Where has it gone? Kern knows that, too, of course: "It was sold. Really!" In the year 1900, the then owner put an advertisement in the newspaper offering Böttinger House for demolition, with – as the wording went – "six magnificent portals, 70 window frames, copious sculptures, balustrades, vases, statues, busts, surmounts and coronas…" Luckily they did not flog the whole house, but broke "only" parts off the façade facing the garden and sold them – but still enough to ornament a whole house, the so-called Bamberger House, in Luitpoldpark in Munich. "I know it," says the lady from Munich, but admits she did not know how it got its name.

Kern tells them to take a look into the stairwell with its wealth of stucco mouldings. "I always feel as if I'm inside a shell here," he says and uses that idea to lead on to the present use of the house as an art gallery. There had been a classy restaurant in the old palais before. It had an affiliated bed and breakfast hotel with rooms in two

"Romanesque Tower", a student hall of residence

restored historical buildings nearby. It could not keep going unfortunately and had to close.

Kern asks his group to follow him on one more, and last, detour to the foot of the Kaulberg, to Pfahlplätzchen. The lovely *House of the Crab*, where the philosopher Hegel lived for about two years, stands in the little square. Hegel edited a newspaper in Bamberg; but the paper he and other great brains produced soon folded. Kern thinks perhaps it was "too good". The group is delighted by the lovely view over the intimate little square and up the Kaulberg to the Upper Parish Church. They go back along Judenstraße as far as Böttinger House, where they fork left into Concordiastraße and then left again to the Upper Mills. They stop on the mill bridge.

Kern recounts that the Upper Mills were one of the most important redevelopment projects in the Old Town. A trust bought the whole complex, which was in ruins. They took great trouble in restoring the parts that could be preserved and replaced those that could not with new buildings. In his opinion, they carried this out with fitting measure and proportions, thereby saving it as an ensemble, not exactly a simple thing to do. "Look behind you," says Kern and points to buildings on the hill side of the river: houses that have not been restored yet.

The group is interested to know how the restored Upper Mills are used now. Kern informs them: they have mostly been converted into halls of residence for students. The new building in the middle of the river, standing between two weirs, is St. Nepomuk's Hotel, named after a statue of the saint on the bridge. "What you can't see, because the Regnitz flows over it, is an underwater power station underneath us," says Kern. "It produces district heating for the city centre and Old Town." A highly welcome project, as there is no emission in the air.

"Now our tour of the town is coming to an end," announces Kern. He walks right through the area of the Upper Mills and on to Mühlwörth, a street along the bank of the Regnitz. On the opposite bank, Böttinger's second "house", the riverside palais named Concordia, seems to rise from the river, in which it is reflected. Before restoration, it housed a state geochemical research institute, which meant there were laboratories under stucco

The philosopher Hegel lived in the "House of the Crab"

ceilings. Now it is the seat of the Villa Concordia International Artists' House. A modern extension with a glass front gives us a clue as to its function. It was set up by the Free State of Bavaria and offers the scholarship holders – painters and sculptors, literary figures and composers – a place to work and live.

As promised, Kern finally shows them an industrial monument, lock number 100 of the old Ludwig Canal by the fulling-mill. The construction, built in 1840, looks like a toy but it is in full working order and is flooded from time to time if a boat wants to go through.

The group turns round and walks back to the Upper Mills. Just before them, they turn right in the direction of Nonnenbrücke, a bridge lead-

ing over the old canal and into Schillerplatz. This is where Kern wants to end his tour. After all, it is late afternoon, almost evening. The municipal theatre, renovated from top to bottom, stands on one side of the square. Rich in tradition, it was founded by a man of the theatre, Count Soden, around 1800. The Romantic writer, E.T.A. Hoffmann, worked there as director of music; he lived and suffered, as Kern puts it, over there in that narrow-fronted house, No. 26 Schillerplatz – a multigenius in the restricted atmosphere of the seat of a small principality recently degraded to the rank of a provincial town. At least he had a publisher – Kunz by name – who had the advantage that his real profession was that of a wine merchant. Kern makes a sweeping gesture with his

Foaming whirlpool near the fulling-mill

Villa Concordia International Artists' House

The E.T.A. Hoffmann House seen through a fish-eye lens

"Undine" window in the E.T.A. Hoffmann House

Gallery of Mirrors in the E.T.A. Hoffmann house

hand: "Just have a look at how lovely the square is again!" The square demonstrates better than any other location in the town, how much effort the townspeople of Bamberg put into preserving their old town – the great, the exalted and monumental but equally the small, the meagre, the unprepossessing. And that exactly is the "secret" of Bamberg, the reason why the town is so beautiful, why knowing it makes one so extremely happy and glad: for the very reason, that the unique, art of European standing, is to be found right alongside the insignificant and the mundane, that what is big and important does not disdain what is small and unimportant and, on the other hand, what is small and unprepossessing is not an insult to the remarkable.

These factors above all were the reasons for Bamberg's Old Town being put on the UNESCO World Heritage list in 1993 – an honour that, by the beginning of this millennium, had been awarded to not even thirty monuments or ensembles in Germany. Bamberg regards the honour as an obligation to preserve its appearance and its historical personality – not as a city that is a museum in itself, but as a vigorous city that has evolved over a thousand years, a town where it is possible to "read" German history, including history of art, in the "original text".

Kern seems almost moved, when he says goodbye: "I'd like to thank you very much indeed for the receptiveness with which you followed me. Thank you for your interest and the appreciation of beauty you showed – you were wonderful. Do remember Bamberg with pleasure or – even better – come back again!" He makes a bow, just as he had bowed to them on the Upper Bridge at the beginning of their *Day for Bamberg*, and shakes hands with all eleven. The lady from Munich, who had turned out to be a bank manager's wife, quickly stands on tiptoe and gives Kern a kiss on the left cheek. "Thank you," she says in a firm voice, "we won't forget you either." Kern waves back to them once more. He goes past the statue of E.T.A. Hoffmann with the tomcat Murr on his shoulder, says: "So long, old boy," and thinks about Julia, the young girl that the poet had an unrequited love for while in Bamberg, and carries the kiss on his left cheek home like a trophy.

Crowns Bamberg's highest hill: Altenburg Castle

Index of Pictures